MAKING VISITORS MINDFUL

Principles for Creating Quality Sustainable Visitor Experiences through Effective Communication

Gianna Moscardo

SAGAMORE PUBLISHING

Champaign, Illinois

www.sagamorepub.com

Interior Layout: Michelle R. Dressen
Cover Design: Julie L. Denzer

ISBN: 1-57167-259-1
Library of Congress Card Catalog Number: 99-62748

Printed in the United States of America.

■ Aim & Scope of Series

ADVANCES IN TOURISM APPLICATIONS provides a new forum for organizing and presenting emerging theory and management practices in five, broadly defined areas of tourism management: (1) destination marketing, (2) destination management, (3) environment, (4) policy, and (5) statistics and theory. This new series of monographs attempts to fill an important gap between textbooks and journal articles, representing a comprehensive discussion of the most current theories and/or practices by leading scholars and industry professionals. Each volume identifies and discusses the most current theories and/or practices relevant to a specific topic, provides concrete examples and explanations of the importance of these theories/practices to the tourism industry, and provides extensive bibliographic resources.

As editors of the series, we want to encourage and facilitate the creativity of researchers and managers in tourism. Specifically, we invite readers to contribute by submitting manuscripts and/or case studies which describe innovative applications in the tourism industry. We welcome your ideas and suggestions for future topics and look forward to joining you on this journey of building knowledge for the 21st century.

• •

Dr. Daniel R. Fesenmaier
Dept. of Leisure Studies
University of Illinois at
Urbana-Champaign
Champaign, IL USA

Dr. Joseph T. O'Leary
Dept. of Forestry &
Natural Resources
Purdue University
W. Lafayette, IN USA

Dr. Musaffer S. Uysal
Dept. of Hospitality and
Tourism Management
Virginia Polytechnic Institute
Blacksburg, VA USA

Other titles currently available in the
Advances in Tourism Applications Series

Acknowledgments

There are many people whose contributions to the writing and production of this book must be acknowledged. Taking them in chronological order, I shall begin by thanking Philip Pearce for introducing me to Ellen Langer's work and to tourism as a serious research topic. Ellen Langer provided the core idea of mindfulness, and although we have never met, her work has provided inspiration both for my own research and for dealing with life in general. Betty Drinkwater, George Kearney, and Glenn Ross all gave me sound advice and good guidance throughout my time as a doctoral student, and with their support, I pursued mindfulness as a path to understanding how visitors respond to information.

Many of the ideas in this book were also developed with the help of various research assistants and graduate students. In particular, I would like to thank Kathryn MacKenzie, Margot Warnett, and Robin Aiello. All three work directly with visitors, and they happily provided thoughts and comments on the practicality of my ideas. Barbara Woods has kept this whole show running for several years and helped the research in too many ways to list. I would also like to thank Amanda Clark, David Green, and Tanya Greenwood, my current research team, for their patience with my many and varied requests.

Professors Chris Crossland and Joe O'Leary are also owed a vote of thanks—Professor O'Leary for suggesting that I write the book, and Professor Crossland for agreeing it would be a worthwhile activity.

Then there is Anne Sharp. Without Anne, very little would ever get done in the Department of Tourism. She is not only brilliant with word processors, but she is always cheerful under pressure, and her unconditional support for everything we do makes us feel important and keeps us going.

Finally, I must thank Tom and Jack for being permanently mindful and also always enthusiastic.

Several of the studies referred to in this book were conducted with funding from the Cooperative Research Centre for Ecologically Sustainable Development of the Great Barrier Reef World Heritage Area, also known as the CRC Reef Research Centre. The CRC Reef Research Centre also provided the funds for part of the author's salary during the writing of this book.

Contents

CHAPTER FOUR
Connecting to Visitors

CHAPTER FIVE
Providing Variety

CHAPTER SIX
Telling a Good Story That Makes Sense

■ 1

Why Do We Need to Be Mindful about Communicating with Visitors?

SAMUEL BUTLER wrote that "exploring is delightful to look forward to ... but it is not comfortable at the time, unless it be of such an easy nature as not to deserve the name" (Fraser, 1991, p. *vii*). As a researcher in the field of tourism and recreation, I find that contemplation of the future brings some sense of hope as I anticipate the potential positive benefits of improved recreation and tourism. But I am also very aware that as we hasten towards the 21st century, it will not be easy to fulfill this potential without much careful consideration and planning by researchers, public managers, and private industry. We must not forget that making tourism and recreation a successful component of life in the next century will not be easy.

Tourism and recreation managers can be viewed as explorers. Like all travelers, they need to prepare for their journeys, taking only what is necessary and learning from the travelers of the past.

Let us begin our expedition by pausing briefly to look back at the tourism world behind us and by considering the lessons that we can learn from the past. The clear and overwhelming lesson from past experience in tourism and recreation is that not everyone has been happy to have guests! Tourism in particular has attracted much criticism, most of which has been concerned with the negative consequences of tourism for the places and people who act as hosts. Jafari (1990), in his history of research into tourism, notes that there is a predominance of a "reactionary platform," which refers to a large group of writers and researchers who have focused attention on the negative social, cultural, economic, and environmental impacts of tourism. Results of negative impacts for travelers have ranged from suffering the hostility of angry residents to the loss of opportunities when communities choose not to develop facilities or infrastructure to allow tourism. Similar concerns about, and responses to, recreational activities can be found.

CHAPTER 1: OVERVIEW

AIMS	MAJOR THEMES	SECTIONS WILL PROVIDE
To introduce the book.	**We need to find ways to make tourism and recreation more sustainable.**	A background to sustainable tourism and recreation. Definitions of the terms used. Advice to readers on how to use the book.
To describe how visitor communication programs can encourage more sustainable tourism and recreation.	**Communication activities can encourage sustainable tourism and recreation by:** 1. **enhancing visitor experiences,** 2. **managing visitors and their impacts.** **To do this we need to be effective at communicating with visitors.**	Examples of how communication can enhance visitor experiences. Examples of how communication can assist in the management of visitors and their impacts.

Let us move from the past to the present and turn our gaze from the world behind us to the world around us. "May you live in interesting times" is an often-quoted Chinese phrase, sometimes used as a curse and sometimes as a challenge. It is certainly true that in the 1990s we are traveling in interesting times, and explorers would do best to see this as a challenge rather than a curse. Certainly the present world is changing at an ever-accelerating pace. More and more people, including large numbers of people from the rapidly developing Asian countries, can and do travel. No longer are travelers the wealthy Westerners who dominated tourism in the first seven decades of this century. This change should make us consider again what travel means, particularly to travelers from other cultures. Increasing leisure time and changing demographics have also created greater demands for, and new patterns of, recreation. Further, both tourists and recreationists are becoming more sophisticated, older, wiser, more diverse, and more concerned with leisure as an integral part of their lives. The balance has changed from leisure as an escape to leisure as an essential part of self-development. There are also new frontiers, new places to travel with the opening of Eastern Europe, and the development of tourism in more remote and harsh places such as Antarctica. We should note that as some places become more open to travel, others are closed. Some of these places are closed because of hostility, such as in the Middle East, but others have been closed, or restricted, because of fears of destruction by visitors.

Technology has also had a remarkable impact on leisure, allowing for easier and more interesting transport options and for development in a variety of places.

Technology, though, can also work against forms of traditional tourism and recreation, offering better leisure experiences that people can have in their own homes. This new reality, virtual reality, could give the phrase "armchair traveler" a whole new meaning. Indeed, in the classic Arnold Schwarzenegger film, *Total Recall*, the plot revolves around the ability to buy a holiday experience which is implanted in your brain. In this *Total Recall* vision of the future, travelers can go nowhere to have great experiences. For those of us who earn our living from tourism, it was heartening to note that these implanted holidays had the potential to go horribly wrong!

From the past, some lessons are clear. Our baggage for the journey into the future of tourism and recreation should respect the diversity of visitors, and recognize the need to manage tourism impacts. The challenge for us as explorers is to find in the future leisure experiences that are rewarding and sustainable for both hosts and guests. The core aim of this book is to describe some principles for ensuring that tourism and recreation in the future provide these rewarding and sustainable experiences. In particular, the book will concentrate on communicating with visitors.

WHAT THIS BOOK IS ABOUT

Communicating with visitors is a common activity in tourism and recreation management. There are many situations in which we need to be able to give visitors information. These situations can range from basic safety messages and simple directions to complex explanations of the cultural or evolutionary history of a place. Giving visitors knowledge is particularly important for activities such as guided tours, visitor information centers, museums, art galleries, zoos, historic buildings and sites, visitor education programs in national parks and other protected environments, and promotional campaigns.

The major aim of this book is to set out a series of principles to assist in communicating with visitors. These principles are applicable to a broad range of tourism and recreation situations. The principles which are described in this book have been derived from both the results of applied research in tourism and recreation settings and from a theory of how people deal with, learn, and use new information. This mindfulness/mindlessness theory of human information processing has been tested and used in a range of business, educational, medical, and other social applications. Its proponent, Harvard University Professor Ellen Langer, has been a recipient of the American Psychological Association's Award for Distinguished Contributions to Psychology in the Public Interest. This award specifically recognizes work which has clear and immediate benefits for applied questions and, in Langer's case, work which is easily accessible to non-psychologists.

Building on Langer's work and on existing and original research, this book offers:

1. Principles and examples relevant and applicable to a broad range of tourism and recreation settings,

2. Directions for the planning, design, and management of educational programs and other visitor communication services which are based on a large body of applied and relevant research evidence, and
3. A theory which is easily accessible to managers and which can be used to generate ideas for communicating with visitors in many different places.

Some Points to Note about the Structure of the Book

The greatest challenge in writing a book about communication is making sure that you take your own advice. The author has to try as hard as possible to use the principles being proposed in the way she designs her own communications. So I have included several features with the aim of making this book flexible and easy to follow.

1. Each chapter is virtually self-contained, with few references made to other chapters. This means you can read each one on its own and mostly in any order you like. This means you can leave out some if you do not think they are relevant or interesting and you can read the book at your leisure.
2. Each chapter has the same basic structure:
   - An introduction to the topic and evidence that it is important.
   - A series of sections describing various aspects of the topic with examples.
   - A conclusion.

   If you are prepared to accept my argument that the topic is important, you can skip the introduction and go straight to the sections with the examples. If you are in a real hurry, you can always go straight to the conclusions.
3. All the chapters, except the last, have an overview which is like a map for the chapter somewhere near the beginning. The overview contains the aims of the chapter, the key messages or major themes, and what is in the sections. Reading the major themes and the conclusions will give you the critical information contained in each chapter.

DEFINITIONS

Before presenting any theory, principles, or examples, it is useful to set out some definitions. An important component of good communication is to ensure that both the communicator and the audience share an understanding of commonly used terms.

Visitors, Tourists, and Recreationists

Firstly, let us consider whom we are talking about. In the introductory section, the phrase "tourism and recreation" was used to describe the focus of the book, suggesting that we are talking about two different types of people—tourists and recreationists. As is typical in many areas, there is much debate in the academic literature over definitions of tourism and recreation. Some would argue that they are basically the same; some wish to see them as very different. For the purposes of this book, a simpler approach will be taken. The term "visitor" will be used to describe people who travel away from their normal places of residence for work, for leisure, or to visit friends and family. This definition includes both people who stay away for the day only and people who stay away overnight. It is an adaptation of the World Tourism Organization's definition of visitors (McIntyre, 1993).

Communication, Interpretation, and Education

So far, the term "communication" has been the major one used when describing what the book is about. The *Concise Oxford Dictionary* uses the following words and phrases to define *communication*, the noun, and *communicate*, the verb:

to impart, transmit; to succeed in conveying information or evoking understanding (and to make a) connection between place (1982, p. 190).

The use of "communication" in this book is consistent with this definition in that it refers to giving information, creating understanding, and making connections between managers and visitors.

A very similar term is that of interpretation. Table 1.1 contains several definitions of "interpretation." There are many parallels between these definitions and the definition of "communication" that has just been outlined. Clearly, "interpretation" is about communicating, but the definitions of "interpretation" also concentrate on the importance of visitor enjoyment, on exciting curiosity and on contributing to conservation. "Interpretation" is a special kind of communication that is particularly relevant to tourism and recreation.

Interpretation, however, is a technical term used in specific ways by select groups and organizations. For this reason, the present book will use both phrases interchangeably and together. It is worth noting that interpretation has also been defined as a type of education, and some readers may be more familiar with the

---

Interpretation is the process of explaining to people the significance of the place or object they have come to see, so that they enjoy their visit more, understand their heritage and environment better, and develop a more caring attitude towards conservation.
(Society for Interpreting Britain's Heritage)

Interpretation is an educational activity which aims to reveal meanings and relationships through the use of original objects, by first-hand experience, and by illustrative media, rather than simply to communicate factual information.
(Tilden, 1977)

The job of interpretation is to open the minds of people so they can receive ... the interesting signals that the world is constantly sending.
(Edwards, 1979*)

Interpretation is a planned effort to create for the visitor an understanding of the history and significance of events, people, and objects with which the site is associated.
(Alderson & Low, 1985*)

---

* Quoted in Knudson *et al.* (1995)

Table 1.1: Some definitions of interpretation

phrase *public or environmental education*. The principles to be described apply equally to education, interpretation, and communication.

GOOD REASONS FOR COMMUNICATING WITH VISITORS

Sustainable Tourism and Recreation

> We're five billion of us on this little earth swimming around in space. And there's too many of us, and most of us are living incorrectly.
> (Turner, quoted in Knudson et al., 1995, p. 475)

This statement succinctly describes the core concerns driving advocates of global sustainability. The essential elements of sustainability are stable human populations, limited growth, long-term maintenance of biological resources, and the maintenance of quality, both specifically in environments and ecosystems, and more generally in people's lives (Brown et al., 1987). "The question is, can five billion people turn it around in time? We're fighting against a deadline for our own survival" (Turner, quoted in Knudson et al., 1995, p. 471).

Communication and interpretation can play a critical role in achieving sustainability. The importance of education in general has been recognized by many authors and organizations concerned with encouraging sustainable practices, and a call for increased education and public awareness is included in documents such as the *Brundtland Report* and the 1992 Earth Summit's *Agenda 21*. For many people, the information they encounter while at leisure may offer the only opportunity to learn about their bonds to the environment, or to their history and culture.

How then can the principles of sustainable development be applied to tourism and recreation? Table 1.2 sets out the key goals and characteristics of sustainable tourism as described in the Australian Government's ESD Working Group Report for Tourism (1991). Lane (1991) expands upon several of the characteristics listed in Table 1.2, in particular, those concerned with social equity and community involvement, regional planning, and the nature and quality of the experience for visitors. He defines sustainable tourism as providing

> satisfying jobs without dominating the local economy. It must not abuse the natural environment, and should be architecturally respectable ... The benefits of tourism should be diffused through many communities, not concentrated on a narrow coastal strip or scenic valley. (1991, p. 2)

Lane also suggests that the quality of the experience for the tourist is critical. Specifically, he states that "the visitor will gain an in-depth understanding and knowledge of the area, its landscapes, and peoples. The tourist will become concerned and, therefore, protective of the host area" (1991, p. 2).

Goals
To improve material and non-material well-being of communities.
To preserve intergenerational and intragenerational equity.
To protect biological diversity and maintain ecological systems.
To ensure the cultural integrity and social cohesion of communities.
Characteristics
Tourism which is concerned with the quality of experience.
Tourism which has social equity and community involvement.
Tourism which operates within the limits of the resource—this includes minimization of impacts and use of energy and the use of effective waste management and recycling techniques.
Tourism which maintains the full range of recreational, educational, and cultural opportunities within and across generations.
Tourism which is based upon activities or designs which reflect the character of a region.
Tourism which allows the guest to gain an understanding of the region visited and which encourages guests to be concerned about, and protective of, the host community and environment.
Tourism which does not compromise the capacity of other industries or activities to be sustainable.
Tourism which is integrated into local, regional, and national plans.

Table 1.2: Goals and characteristics of ecologically sustainable tourism

In summary then, sustainable tourism is based upon three core principles:
1. Quality. Sustainable tourism provides a quality experience for visitors, while improving the quality of life of the host community and protecting the quality of the environment (Inskeep, 1991).
2. Continuity. Sustainable tourism ensures the continuity of the natural resources upon which it is based and the continuity of the culture of the host community and requires continuity of visitor interest (Wall, 1993).
3. Balance. Sustainable tourism balances the needs of hosts, guests, and the environment (Bramwell and Lane, 1993; Nitsch and van Straaten, 1995).

Good communication or interpretation can contribute to sustainable tourism and recreation through:
- enhancing the quality of the experience for visitors and encouraging continued visitor interest in the activity, and
- assisting in the management of visitors and their impacts, thus contributing to the continued quality of the environment and way of life of the host community.

Enhancing Visitor Experience

There are three main ways that communication and interpretation can contribute to the quality of visitors' experience. These are:

1. Providing information on alternatives and options,
2. Providing information to encourage safety and comfort, and
3. Creating the actual experience.

Alternatives and Options

In tourism and recreation, satisfaction is usually seen as resulting from a positive match between the visitors' expectations and the experiences available (Kotler et al., 1996; Driver et al., 1987). In other words, enjoyment comes from a good match between what the visitor wants and what the destination offers. One way to encourage such a match is to provide visitors with good information about the available options so that they can make the best choices about what they do and where they go.

Mack and Thompson (1991) provide an example of the value of providing information to assist visitors in the wise use of their time in the United States' Rocky Mountain National Park. These authors describe the process of visitor research undertaken to support the redevelopment of exhibits in the Kawuneeche Visitor Center situated on the U.S. Highway 34 entrance on the western side of the Rocky Mountain National Park.

The first step in the research was a survey which identified both the various activities that visitors were seeking and the time they had available to spend in the park. Three main types of visitors were identified: half-day visitors, full-day visitors, and multiple-day visitors. The major objective of the new exhibits was to help visitors make the best choices about the activities they were interested in, and to match the time they had available. To meet this objective, each exhibit was dedicated to a particular activity such as birdwatching, photography, or fishing, and information in the exhibit was presented in five color bands. One color presented options for half-day visitors, one color gave information on alternatives for full-day visitors, while a third color offered options for multiple-day visitors. A fourth color was used to highlight basic information relevant to all visitors, and a fifth color outlined an invitation to gather further information. Figure 1.1 is a plan of one of the exhibits which demonstrates the five-color system.

The second step in the research process was to evaluate the impact of the new information center design on visitors. This evaluation suggested that the design was an effective one, with substantial increases in activity participation suggesting easier access and improved knowledge of options. There were also substantial decreases in various visitor concerns, indicating improved effectiveness in the communication of information. Finally, sales of park publications and guidebooks increased by 50 percent. According to the authors, "the increase in sales figures was a nice benefit, but the more important accomplishment is the constant reminder that these publications provide information to visitors about the park and the environment" (p. 115).

Bird-Watching	The pristine and diverse habitats of Rocky Mountain National Park are home to some 250 species of birds. Patterns of bird life reveal themselves as you watch from a quiet vantage point. Seeing a hawk soar or a kingfisher getting a meal can be an unforgettable experience for young and old alike.	Layer 1 Neutral-Colored Introduction
Occasional stops along Trail Ridge Road will reveal several of the park's many bird species. Watch for green-tailed towhees in the sagebrush flats and mountain bluebirds in the open meadows. [Several other species & locations are described.] △1	Illustrations of people bird-watching	Layer 2 Light Color for Short Stays
With a full day to spend in the park, you can enjoy the hike to Lulu City through a variety of good birding habitats. The trail starts at 9,000 feet (2,743m) and runs parallel to the Colorado River and its beaver ponds. Mallard ducks are frequently seen around the water, and you might observe a dipper on a rock in mid-stream. [Text continues to describe several species.] ☐2	Illustrations of species	Layer 3 Darker Color for Day Visits
An extended stay allows you to spend more time in the mountain meadows, subalpine forest, and alpine tundra. A sharp eye and a little luck might lead you to an osprey feeding on brook trout in the Kawuneeche Valley, where marsh hawks also make their home. [Again more examples are given.] ○3	More illustrations	Layer 4 Dark Color for Overnight Visits
CASE CONTAINING BOOKS		Layer 5 Options for Detailed Information

Figure 1.1: Plan or outline of a Kawuneeche Visitor Centre exhibit

Comfort and Safety

It is interesting to note that in the Rocky Mountain National Park research, many of the visitors' concerns were about safety and comfort issues. While safety messages may often be included in tourism and recreation communications, there is little evidence that they are effective or informative. Figure 1.2 is a replica of the crocodile warning sign used in national parks and other public areas in Queensland, Australia. This particular sign was chosen after a major research program evaluated schoolchildren's responses to various versions of a warning sign. The research found significant differences in people's perceptions of the messages given by the signs. Responses to some of the alternatives included statements such as "crocodiles only swim in tunnels" and "you can swim here because there are crocodiles" (Pearce, 1982a). Clearly, not all safety or warning messages work.

Even less attention has been paid to comfort issues. Even simple advice can make a large difference in the quality of the visitor experience. An example helps highlight this issue. The author was once in charge of a tourism-management student field trip to the various national parks of the Far Northern region of Australia's eastern coastline. At one particular park, the Edmund Kennedy National Park, we decided to go on a mangrove boardwalk which was recommended by a local ranger. The boardwalk was certainly as impressive as described, taking us through a variety of coastal, mangrove, and melaleuca swamplands. Unfortunately, the overwhelming memory of that experience for all the participants were the clouds of hungry mosquitoes who vigorously attacked and pursued us. A simple warning to make

Figure 1.2: The most effective crocodile warning sign

liberal use of an insect repellent would have changed the nature of this experience quite dramatically.

Creating the Experience

In many tourism and recreation settings, communication or interpretation is either an important component of the experience or is the experience. In guided walks and tours, self-guided trails, ecotours, art galleries, fauna sanctuaries, and zoos, for example, interpretation and education are major components of the experience offered. Not only are these important and popular activities, but there is evidence that interest in educational leisure activities is increasing.

Recent commentaries on trends in tourism and leisure have emphasized several factors related to this increased interest in educational leisure. Poon (1993) notes the following trends in tourism:

- growing demand for independent travel arrangements and a declining growth rate for traditional package tours,
- increasing differentiation in lifestyles and correspondingly increasing differentiation in types of visitors,
- greater demand for choice and flexibility,
- rising use of information technologies in travel planning, and
- changes in the motivation of tourists.

According to Poon, new tourists "are more experienced travelers, more educated, more destination-oriented, more independent, more flexible and more green" (1993, p. 18). Urry (1990) has outlined similar trends and changes in leisure and patterns of consumption. He goes on to link this increasing interest in education to the expansion of museums and heritage attractions in Britain.

These arguments are supported by research evidence. Table 1.3, for example, lists the five most important travel motivation items for international and domestic tourists visiting a high-profile tourist region in Australia. The first column lists the responses given by 1,600 visitors to a survey conducted in 1994; the second column lists the responses given by 1,400 visitors to a similar survey conducted two years later. In both cases, "learning new things and increasing my knowledge" is a very important motivation. It was more important than having fun, escaping the demands of home, indulging in luxury, and being physically active.

If visitors are increasingly seeking educational elements across all aspects of their travel, we can expect greater emphasis being placed on communication and interpretation as integral parts of the visitor experience available at various tourist and recreation sites. Pearce (1991) provides two cases where the experience provided relies almost solely on the physical setting. These are Stonehenge and Niagara Falls. In both examples, there is little interpretation available to provide visitors with the understanding they need to appreciate these places. As a result, Stonehenge received the lowest visitor enjoyment scores of 13 major English historic sites in a survey research program aimed at understanding visitor satisfaction. Similarly, one-third of visitors surveyed at Niagara Falls were critical about the experience, particularly the provision of information.

1994 Survey (n = 1600)		1996 Survey (n = 1400)	
Motive	Mean Score*	Motive	Mean Score*
See outstanding scenery	1.5	Learn new things or increase knowledge	1.5
Have nice weather	1.6	See a foreign place	1.6
Experience new and different lifestyles	1.65	Have fun or be entertained	1.7
Learn new things or increase knowledge	1.7	Get a change from a busy life	1.75
Get away from the demands of home	1.8	Get away from the demands of home	1.8

*Scale went from 1—always important, to 4—never important.
Data were collected by CRC Reef Research.
The samples were comparable and the same motivation items were tested. The 1996 survey, however, used a shorter list of terms.

Table 1.3: Five most important travel motives for visitors surveyed in North and Far North Queensland

By way of contrast, we can examine three cases where greater effort has been put into communicating with visitors. The first is a study of commercial whitewater rafting trips conducted in West Virginia's New River Gorge National River (Roggenbuck and Williams, 1991). In this case, the National Park Service began a program to encourage commercial river-tour operators to provide more information to visitors. One component of this was the provision of seminars to increase guides' knowledge of the natural and cultural history and national significance of the area. The researchers studied the impact of this program by surveying visitors before and after it was implemented. Roggenbuck and Williams concluded that their results showed "that customers who went on their trip after guide training received significantly more interpretation and derived much more knowledge of the area and enjoyment from the trip" (1991, p. 6) than did visitors surveyed before the guide-training program.

The Blists Hill Museum at Ironbridge Gorge Museum in the United Kingdom provides our second case (Beeho and Prentice, 1995). Ironbridge Gorge is a World Heritage site famous for its buildings, construction, and artifacts, which provide an insight into the Industrial Revolution. Rather than present these historical relics in a static, conventional museum, the management of the Blists Hill area has created an open-air, or living, museum. This living museum recreates parts of the Gorge as they were in the nineteenth century and uses costumed interpreters to provide information to visitors. As in the previous case, a research study was conducted to gain an understanding of visitor responses. Again, interpretation was found to be a critical component of the visitor experience. The two most frequently given benefits of visiting Blists Hill Open-Air Museum were "having a good day out" and "the satisfaction of having learnt something new" (Beeho and Prentice, 1995, p. 243). The authors further noted that "in the main, visitors liked to have people tell them how everything worked and to give them background information about each exhibit" (p. 240).

The final case is that of the Skyrail Rainforest Cableway, which takes visitors on a gondola trip above the canopy of the Wet Tropics World Heritage rainforests of North Eastern Australia (Woods and Moscardo, 1996). Unlike many other scenic cableways, which provide a mostly passive opportunity to view scenery, the management of Skyrail has invested heavily in interpretation. The three core elements of this interpretation are a rainforest boardwalk with information signs, a rainforest information center, and a staff of trained guides who provide both tours and on-the-spot commentaries.

The author was part of a team which conducted a series of visitor surveys aimed at evaluating the contribution of Skyrail's communication program to its visitors' experiences. Overall visitors' satisfaction with their trip on Skyrail was high. The mean score for overall satisfaction was 8.7 on a scale of 1 (not at all satisfied) to 10 (extremely satisfied). Ratings on individual components of the experience, such as service, value for money, efficiency of staff, friendliness of staff, and information on the rainforest, were also high. These high satisfaction scores were supported by the fact that the majority of visitors intended to return to Skyrail sometime in the future if they had the opportunity. For international visitors, 62% would visit Skyrail again if they returned to North Queensland and, for Australian visitors residing outside North Queensland, 75% indicated an intention to return to Skyrail.

Local residents were an interesting group in terms of intention to return, because they have easy access to the attraction. Local residents can be the harshest critics of local attractions, yet they act as tour guides to friends and relatives who visit the area. Their satisfaction and intention to return is therefore a useful way to gauge the success of a tourist attraction. This group also indicated a positive intention to return, with 42% intending to return within the next 12 months and a further 11% intending to return after 12 months. These results indicated that visitors enjoyed their Skyrail experience. But did interpretation have any influence on satisfaction, or would visitors be just as satisfied from the gondola ride alone? From a tourism perspective, is there actually any point to providing visitors with a learning experience? The results indicated that the interpretation was an important component of satisfaction. Visitors who experienced any of the three interpretive components were significantly more satisfied with their experience than those who simply rode on the cableway. This particular study also examined the effectiveness of the Skyrail communication program in increasing visitors' knowledge about the rainforest. Again, the results were positive. Visitors who participated in any of the three interpretive activities offered had significantly higher scores on several indicators of rainforest knowledge.

In addition to impacts on learning and rainforest knowledge, the researchers were also interested in the impacts that the Skyrail experience might have on planned rainforest activities. Table 1.4 provides a comparison of the pre-visit and post-visit samples in terms of their intentions to engage in various rainforest activities available in the region. Skyrail appears to have decreased visitor intentions for most other activities, and this was especially the case for short rainforest walks, wildlife viewing, and rainforest day trips. If these changed intentions translate into changes in actual behaviors, then it is very likely that the Skyrail experience will lessen pressure on other heavily used sites which usually provide short rainforest walks and are commonly used by day-trip operations.

Managing Visitors and Their Impacts

The Skyrail case study demonstrated the potential for communication to change or influence visitor behavior. It is this potential that provides the second good reason for communicating with visitors: managing their impacts. There are two main ways communication can contribute to visitor management:

1. Influencing where visitors go, and
2. Informing visitors about appropriate behaviors.

Influencing Where Visitors Go

This function of communication is the management parallel to providing options to enhance visitor experience. In the previous section, the emphasis was on matching visitors to activities to encourage satisfaction. In this section, the emphasis is on providing information which can influence where visitors go and thus assist in managing their impacts. The most common approach is providing information about alternative sites, routes, or activities as an attempt to move visitors away from heavily used sites. The argument is that such a strategy will help manage

Activity	% of Pre-Visit Sample	% of Post-Visit Sample
Short rainforest walks*	75%	25%
Wildlife viewing*	65%	35%
Rainforest day trips*	64%	36%
Canoeing	56%	44%
National park sightseeing	54%	46%
Bird-watching	54%	46%
Overnight rainforest walks	51%	49%
Rainforest day walks	46%	54%
Bush walking	48%	52%

*Significant differences at the 0.05 level indicated by Goodman and Kruskal's Taus.

Table 1.4: Intentions to engage in rainforest activities for pre-visit and post-visit skyrail samples

negative impacts at those sites under the most pressure. Coleman (1997) provides examples of this type of management strategy being used in various English national parks. The Lake District Traffic Management Initiative, for example, is a program designed to alleviate crowding problems by encouraging the use of secondary roads and alternative transport modes. One of the methods being used is an information program.

Roggenbuck (1992) also provides evidence from several studies in the United States that information on high-use areas and alternative sites or routes can positively influence visitor behavior. Huffman and Williams (1987), for example, tested the impact of a computer information display on the trail choices of back-country hikers in the Rocky Mountains National Park. Without the information, about 17 percent of hikers chose one of 29 alternative trails. With the information, 60 percent selected one of the 29 trails. In another study of a computer information display, similar results were reported (Hultsman, 1988). Ninety-one percent of the surveyed visitors to the Great Smoky Mountains National Park who used the computers reported using their new itinerary, with 85 percent stating that the itinerary improved their visit.

An extension of this function is the use of interpretation as a substitution experience which acts to satisfy visitors without their actually going to the site. The Skyrail case provides an example. By providing a rewarding rainforest experience, Skyrail appears likely to lessen the number of visitors going to other, more sensitive and heavily used sites. The Tyrrell Museum of Paleontology in Alberta, Canada, offers a more complete substitution experience. This large museum offers a variety of interactive displays, audiovisual presentations, and displays of dinosaurs which aim to provide an informative experience of the dinosaurs, whose fossils can be found in the Dinosaur Provincial Park. This world-heritage listed site is very fragile and unable to sustain even limited visitor pressure. The Tyrrell Museum relieves this pressure by providing a substitute experience at an alternative site.

Informing visitors about appropriate behavior

> *The damage tourism causes to the people, economy, and environment of the host area, especially in the long-term, remains hidden from the tourist. He has been left out of all discussion on the subject, even though he is one of the main protagonists ... They are therefore carefree and ignorant rather than devious. To lay all blame at their door would be as wrong as denying their responsibility. But they should certainly be made aware of the situation!*
>
> *(Krippendorf, 1987, p. 43)*

Krippendorf's argument here is a simple one: if you want people to behave in a certain way, then you should tell them. This may seem like common sense, but it is not always the case that tourism or recreation managers provide information on appropriate behavior to visitors. Table 1.5 summarizes the results of research conducted in the Wet Tropics World Heritage rainforests in Australia. This table con-

What visitors want to know	What signs tell them
Conservation issues (50%) Including: - threats to rainforest (11%) - response to damage (13%) - what visitors can do to protect rainforest (20%)	Noting that there are rare/endangered species (16%) Clearing/farming (5%) Response to damage (3% on cyclones) Site-specific behavior (5%) More general, minimal impact behavior (0%)
Rainforest ecology (39%)	Rainforest ecology (72%)
Specific plants/animals (36%)	Specific plants/animals (83%)
Human interaction (13%)	Aboriginal and European history (24%)

Table 1.5: Matching visitor information needs with interpretive content

trasts responses from visitors to questions about the information they wanted with the information actually provided by 89 interpretive signs in the region. The single most common type of question visitors had was about rainforest conservation and how they should behave. Only four signs gave them any information on minimal impact or appropriate behaviors (Moscardo, 1996).

Communication can assist visitors to learn about and use appropriate behavior. Roggenbuck (1992) provides a review of several studies conducted in natural environments which evaluated the impact of various communication techniques on visitor knowledge and attitudes. Table 1.6 provides a summary of the results of this research. In most cases, the communication activity tested was effective in increasing knowledge and, in some cases, creating more favorable attitudes and changing behavior. But Roggenbuck notes that not all versions of the various communication programs were successful with all visitors.

Simply providing information is not by itself likely to result in improved behaviors. Visitors need to have knowledge about both the impacts of various behaviors and the appropriate alternatives; and they need to care about the visited place. One method for developing this care ethic is to provide positive and memorable experiences. Additionally, communication and interpretive efforts have to be effective. They have to make visitors mindful.

WHY DO WE NEED EFFECTIVE COMMUNICATION?

We need effective communication to help us make tourism and recreation more sustainable. In a time of increasing leisure and opportunities to travel, we need to be able to enhance visitor experiences and to assist managers to deal with the pressures and problems created by increasing visitor numbers. Effective communication with visitors can help managers by directing visitors to choose activities

Study	Location	Method	Main Findings
Fazio (1979)	Rocky Mountain National Park	Brochure Trailhead sign Slide show	The slide show, slide show and brochure, and slide show and sign were all associated with significant increases in knowledge about low-impact camping practice and park rules. Visitors who saw the information on park rules were significantly more likely to observe them.
Gallup (1981)	Not given	Cartoon brochures on camping rules	Knowledge scores were significantly higher for those visitors who read the brochure.
Olsen et al. (1984)	4 Ohio State Nature Reserves	Brochures Signs Presentations Guided tours on management policies and rules	All the methods were associated with improved knowledge and more favorable attitudes.
Dowell and McCool (1986)	Missoula Forest	Slide show Booklet on minimal-impact behavior	All methods were associated with significant increases in knowledge. Booklets with the slide show and the slide show alone were associated with more positive attitudes. All methods increased intentions to use low-impact behaviors.
Manfredo and Bright (1991)	Boundary Waters Canoe Area Wilderness	Brochure on appropriate behavior	The brochure was effective for visitors with low levels of knowledge.
Oliver et al. (1985)	Forest Campgrounds	Brochure and Ranger presentation on litter.	The information program decreased littering behavior.
Vanderstoep and Gramann (1987)	Shiloh National Military Park	Information Program	The program did result in reduced impacts.

Note: Details were taken from Roggenbuck (1992).

Table 1.6: Summary of selected communication evaluation studies

wisely, by creating positive and rewarding experiences, by informing visitors about appropriate behavior, and by creating careful, rather than careless, visitors. We need mindful visitors.

So, as explorers, we know what we are looking for. We are searching for ways to make visitors mindful, and for practices and principles that we can bring back to our own places and use to create sustainable and rewarding visitor experiences.

■ 2

Basic Principles for Encouraging Mindful Visitors

A T THE END of the previous chapter I said that if we see ourselves as explorers, the things we need to find are principles to create mindful visitors. But what is a mindful visitor? How will we know when we find one? This chapter describes the concepts of mindfulness and mindlessness and relates them to communication. The chapter ends by setting out some basic principles for effective communication.

CHAPTER 2: OVERVIEW

AIMS	MAJOR THEMES	SECTIONS WILL PROVIDE
1. To introduce the concepts of mindfulness and mindlessness.	**Mindful visitors actively think about where they are and what they are doing. They create new routines for their behaviour and they are more likely to learn new information, change attitudes and behavior, and to enjoy themselves.**	A description of mindlessness and mindfulness. A mindfulness model for communicating with visitors. Some visitor research to support this mindfulness model.
2. To relate mindfulness and mindlessness to communication.	**We can combine what we know about mindfulness, what we know from communication theory and research, and what we know from visitor studies to create a set of basic principles for encouraging mindful visitors and creating effective communication.**	Some results from persuasive communication research. Some thoughts from visitors. A set of principles.
3. To present the basic principles for encouraging mindful visitors.		

The world is full of stories of people being mindless. Take, for example, this story told recently by a work colleague:

My wife asked me to drop our baby son at her mother's on my way to work. The plan was for Grandma to mind the baby for the day while my wife finished working on the final corrections to her doctoral thesis. I don't usually take the baby anywhere on a weekday. So anyway, I put the baby in his car seat in the back of the car and headed off to work as usual. But once I started driving I just followed my usual routine and drove straight to work. It wasn't until I parked the car at work and went to get my briefcase from behind me that I remembered the baby!! I had to get back in the car and drive back to his grandparents'.

Or, another example from a neighbor:

I did the most stupid thing today. I thought my car had been stolen. I left work and went to the floor in the carpark where I usually park and the car wasn't there!! I panicked and called the police to tell them that someone had stolen my car. So they came to the carpark and started asking me questions about what sort of car it was and what color, and if I was sure that this was where I'd left it. And I said, "of course this is where I left it, I always park on this floor." Just then I remembered that I'd been running late that morning and my usual parking space was taken so I had to go up to the next floor. So we walked upstairs and there was my car. I was so embarrassed!! But the policeman said it happens all the time.

These are both ordinary, everyday occurrences of mindlessness. Ellen Langer, in her book entitled *Mindfulness* (1989), gives a much more serious example in her description of the events that resulted in a 1985 Air Florida accident in which seventy-four passengers were killed:

It was a routine flight from Washington, D.C., to Florida with an experienced flight crew. Pilot and copilot were in excellent physical health. Neither was tired, stressed, or under the influence. What went wrong? An extensive examination pointed to the crew's pretakeoff control checks. As the copilot calls out each control on his list, the pilot makes sure the switches are where he wants them to be. One of these controls is an anti-icer. On this day, the pilot and copilot went over each of the controls as they had always done. They went through their routine and checked "off" when the anti-icer was mentioned. This time, however, the flight was different from their experience. This time they were not flying in the usual warm Southern weather. It was icy outside. As he went through the control checks, one by one as he always did, the pilot appeared to be thinking when he was not.

MINDLESSNESS VERSUS MINDFULNESS

Each of these three stories presents an example of mindlessness. In its popular use, we would tend to see mindlessness as a lack of thought. This is not, however, entirely accurate. It is not that the person is not thinking at all. He is not thinking about the new or additional information. In all three examples, the people followed a familiar, often repeated routine or script. Once the routine or script was started, they were unable to change it. Mindlessness therefore can be defined as a way of thinking about the world that relies on existing behavior routines and/or categories, and which limits an individual's ability to recognize and process new information (adapted from Alexander et al., 1989).

> *Mindfulness is the opposite state to mindlessness and can be defined as a "mode of functioning through which the individual actively engages in reconstructing the environment through creating new categories or distinctions, thus directing attention to new contextual cues that may be consciously controlled."*
>
> *(Alexander et al., 1989, p. 951)*

In simpler terms, when we are mindful, we pay attention to the world around us. We can react to new information; we can create new categories for information, new ways of seeing the world, and new routines or scripts for behavior. Mindfulness is a necessary requirement for learning new information. It has also been found to be associated with better decision making, increased self-esteem, and better health (Langer, 1989). Mindlessness, however, is associated with poor judgement, feelings of incompetence, poor health, and boredom. Clearly, in any tourism or recreation setting, our preference would be to encourage visitors to be mindful. The purpose of this chapter is to describe mindfulness and to introduce some basic principles for mindful communication.

It is important to stress that mindlessness and mindfulness refer to different ways of thinking, not just different amounts of thinking. Langer and her associates have shown that people can be mindless even in quite complex situations and that there are at least three paths to mindlessness. The first is the one which was demonstrated in the three examples given at the beginning of this chapter—mindless use of a familiar and/or repetitive routine or script. The second situation is where we accept a given definition or description of the situation which then guides our behavior. In one study, for example (Langer and Newman, 1979), psychology students were randomly assigned to groups and given a handout describing a speaker as cold or as warm. After listening to the speaker, the students were given a questionnaire which tested their recall of the content of the talk and elicited ratings of the speaker. It was hypothesized that students who had better recall of the content, the mindful students, would be less likely to conform to the label given to the speaker. The results confirmed this hypothesis and suggested that mindlessness was related to the acceptance of labels. This supported the results of a previous study

(Langer and Abelson, 1974) of clinical psychologists and their judgement of an interviewee labelled as either a job applicant or a patient. The label "patient" resulted in more negative judgements from the clinicians than the label "job applicant." The people in these situations were mindless because they relied on a pre-existing stereotype to guide their behavior, rather than the information actually available. When people use stereotypes, they are borrowing a routine or script from another situation.

There are a series of puzzles which rely heavily on this type of mindlessness. In the game MindTrap, there is a series of cards which ask questions such as:

> *Kerry Queen, a professional writer, was sitting in his cabin writing a letter. Suddenly Kerry died. How did he die?*
> or
> *There is an ancient invention still used in some parts of the world today that allows people to see through walls. What is it?*

The answer to the first is often difficult for people because they begin their solutions with a definition of "cabin" as a dwelling of some sort. This leads to answers such as "he was eaten by a bear" or "a fire burnt down the cabin." But if we are mindful and think about alternative perspectives on, or definitions of "cabin," we are more likely to get the required answer: "He died in a plane crash. Kerry Queen was a professional skywriter." The same is true for the second quiz. Few of us would define a "window" as "an ancient invention that allows people to see through walls."

Another pathway to mindlessness is through deciding that the information available in a situation is not important or relevant. Chanowitz and Langer (1981) conducted an experiment in which people were given information about two fictitious perceptual disorders, after being told either that the disorders were common or that they were rare. Thus one group believed it unlikely that they would be personally affected by these disorders and, therefore, that the information given was irrelevant to them. Subsequently, all the people were told that they had one of the disorders. Further testing indicated that the people who believed that the information given was irrelevant had not processed it and were unable to use it. Those people who believed that they could be affected had much greater recall of the information about the problem and its treatment.

Now that we know the various pathways to mindlessness, it is worth considering the factors or conditions that encourage mindfulness. The examples previously described give us several options. The study about perceptual disorders tells us that people are more likely to be mindful when the situation is seen as an important one, or the information is personally relevant. We are also more likely to be mindful in new or unfamiliar situations, particularly those where we cannot borrow a script or a routine from somewhere else.

Changing, dynamic situations also encourage mindfulness because it is difficult to develop a routine to follow in a constantly changing set of circumstances.

Such circumstances require us to make decisions, and decision making usually requires some mindful processing of information. Giving people control in a situation both requires decision making and makes the situation and its outcome more important. Not surprisingly, such a combination is an effective method for encouraging mindfulness. The most famous of Langer's studies in psychology was a series of projects conducted with aged residents in a nursing home. In the first study (Langer and Rodin, 1976), some residents were given control over various aspects of their routines and lives and encouraged to be mindful. Comparisons with a group given no control indicated that the mindful group was more alert, active, and happy, and in a follow-up study conducted 18 months later (Rodin and Langer, 1977), 13 out of 44 participants in the no-control group had died, as compared to 7 out of 47 in the mindful group.

Perhaps the biggest challenge to mindfulness, however, is the use of limited definitions or stereotypes. One method to avoid this problem is to encourage people to take an alternative perspective, to think about the world as somebody else might see it. Alternatively, people can explicitly be asked to be mindful. Langer and her colleagues have shown that this latter option can work (Langer et al., 1985). One study of this type of mindfulness training involved asking children to write several answers to a series of questions about the potential skills of people with various disabilities. A comparable, low-mindfulness group of children was asked to provide only a single answer. Various measures were then taken, including a measure of avoidance of disabled people, and judgment of activities that disabled people might be able to participate in. It was found that the high-mindfulness group made fewer inappropriate judgments and were less likely to avoid the target disabled individuals than the low-mindfulness group.

The author has conducted a study which demonstrates the power of both directly asking people to think mindfully about a topic and asking them to take someone else's perspective on a problem or a decision (Moscardo, 1997). The project was done with two classes of undergraduate, tourism-management students divided into several experimental and control groups. One group of students was given the following set of exercises:

> *I would like you to think of yourself as the manager or director of a regional tourist authority whose responsibilities include promotion and development of the tourist products available in your region. You have been asked by your board of directors to consider opportunities in your region for the "seniors" market, or people over the age of 65. The following questions are about the development of activities for this group of visitors.*
> 1. *Make a list of tourist activities or experiences that you believe could be appropriate for "senior" travelers.*
> 2. *Can you think of any advantages that "senior" travelers have over other travelers for enjoying their holidays? Please list them below.*
> 3. *Can you now list below any restrictions that might exist for "senior" travelers?*

4. *Finally, I would like you to imagine yourself as a "senior" traveler and write a paragraph which describes your ideal holiday. Remember, this is your ideal holiday for when you are 65 years or older.*

Another group acted as a full control and was given no training at all. A third group was asked to do the same activities as listed above, but in this case the label "seniors" was removed and the students were asked to describe their own ideal holiday and to list the activities that they would enjoy. Thus, one group was asked to do nothing at all; one group was asked to think about a general tourism problem from their own perspectives; and one group was asked both to think about a problem and to take an alternative perspective.

All three groups were then asked to answer the following questions:

1. *I would like you to consider the region that you have been studying in the previous practicals and design a two-day tour in your region for a small group (8–12 people) of "senior" visitors. Write out the itinerary below, and include information on the type of transport you would use, the accommodations, the places to be visited, and the activities that would be available.*

2. *Now I would like you to think about another group of visitors to your region, the "disabled." I would like you to think about the activities and experiences available in your region and list below any problems that the disabled and their families might have in enjoying a holiday in your region. Please include both the physically and intellectually disabled in your list.*

3. *I would like you now to suggest some solutions to the problems you have listed previously for "disabled" visitors and their families.*

4. *Finally, I would like you to write a mock-up of a small brochure listing activities and experiences that visitors to your region could enjoy when the weather is bad. That is, imagine your region is likely*

---

1. The training and alternatives group listed significantly more activities in its senior traveler itineraries than either of the other groups.

2. Both the training and alternatives and the training-only groups included a significantly broader range of options in their senior traveler itineraries.

3. The training and alternatives group included significantly more nighttime activities for senior travelers.

4. The training and alternatives group identified both more problems and more solutions for disabled travelers.

5. The training and alternatives group suggested more activities for poor weather.

Table 2.1: Summary of mindfulness training for tourism managers study

to experience extended periods of rain and/or cold weather and that you must advise visitors on what they can do in your region during these times.

The responses given to these questions were coded on a variety of features. Table 2.1 summarizes the results of the study. Overall, the group with the training which included taking an alternative perspective demonstrated more flexible and less stereotyped thinking about a range of tourist situations and came up with more solutions to potential problems.

Summary

At this point it is useful to summarize Langer's work on mindfulness/mindlessness. Her work began with the proposition that much complex social behavior can be, and is, conducted mindlessly, or with minimal information processing. According to Langer, in familiar or repetitive situations, a particular aspect of the setting acts as a cue for a script which is then used to guide behavior. Mindlessness can also be triggered in seemingly novel situations in two ways. In one instance, individuals may be able to use labels or cues which allow them to borrow a script from elsewhere, while in the other, individuals may make an initial decision that the information is irrelevant and not engage in any further information processing.

Mindfulness, on the other hand, involves active information processing and the creation of new categories and routines. Mindfulness is likely to occur in novel or unfamiliar situations where no script exists, when a script is interrupted, or where considerable effort or cost to the individual is involved. Table 2.2 provides a summary of the key features of mindfulness and mindlessness.

MINDFULNESS	MINDLESSNESS
Key Features: Open to learning Attention to the setting Development of new routines	**Key Features:** Use of existing routines Little attention to the setting No learning
Conditions: New and different settings Varied and changing situations Control and choice Personal relevance	**Conditions:** Familiar settings Repetitive situations Little control, few choices No personal relevance
Outcomes: Learning and recall Feelings of control Ability to deal with problems Feelings of achievement Feelings of satisfaction	**Outcomes:** No learning, poor recall Feelings of helplessness Limited ability to deal with problems Feelings of incompetence Feelings of dissatisfaction

Table 2.2: Key features of mindfulness and mindlessness

A MINDFULNESS MODEL FOR COMMUNICATING WITH VISITORS

If communication and interpretation are going to be effective tools to enhance experiences and assist in managing tourism and recreation impacts, then mindfulness should be stimulated. Sustainable tourism and recreation are most likely to result from visitors who are active, interested, questioning, and capable of reassessing the way they view the world. Figure 2.1 outlines a mindfulness model of visitor behavior in tourism and recreation settings. This model suggests that two sets of factors influence visitors: Communication and Visitor Factors. Communication Factors refer to the features of the communication or interpretation offered and can be applied to tours, signs, talks, displays, or brochures. Visitor Factors refer to things that visitors bring with them to the tourist or recreation setting. The two sets of factors combine to determine whether visitors will be mindful or mindless. Mindful visitors will be more likely than mindless visitors to enjoy their visit, express satisfaction, learn more, and be interested in discovering more about a topic or place. Mindful visitors should also be more aware of the consequences of their behavior and more appreciative of the heritage site.

The model proposes that the two sets of factors, Communication Factors and Visitor Factors, can combine in a number of ways to produce the visitor's cognitive state. For example, a visitor with a very high level of interest in a topic may be mindful regardless of the Setting Factors, while a visitor who has no interest at all in a topic and who is fatigued may be mindless regardless of the Setting Factors. A visitor with low levels of interest, however, may become mindful in a setting with a variety of experiences and the opportunity to interact with exhibits.

Thus far, the discussion has included both sets of factors as the model aims to provide a complete picture of visitor responses to interpretation and communication. Since setting factors are, however, those that are under the most direct control of site managers, the rest of this section will focus on these factors only. Before doing so, it is important to recognize that there is overlap between the categories set out in Figure 2.1. This is particularly the case for the variables of visitor interest in a topic or place and visitor fatigue. While visitors bring their own interests and experiences with them to any specific place, these do not remain constant throughout their visit. In this model it is argued that it is possible to generate interest in a topic on-site by making connections to visitors' own experiences.

Managers can also consider and influence visitor fatigue through the provision of seating and the programming of tours.

Evidence for the Mindfulness Model

There exists nearly 100 years of research into visitors and how they respond to communication efforts in various tourist and recreation settings. We can look at the results of this research to see if they are consistent with the predictions that are made about communication in the Mindfulness Model.

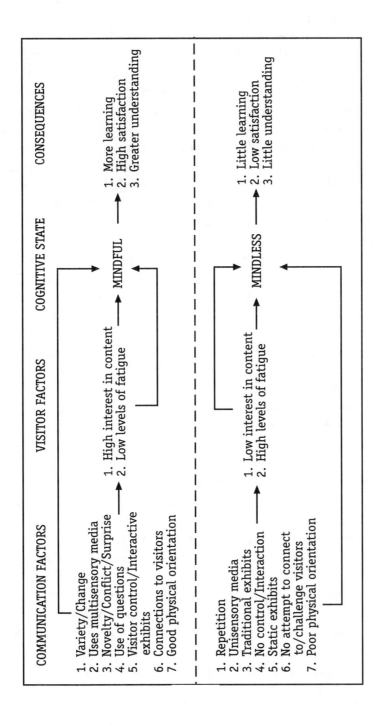

Figure 2.1: Mindfulness model for communicating with visitors

Variety

The first prediction is that variety of experiences encourages mindfulness, while repetition is a pathway to mindlessness. The latter pattern is commonly found in studies which observe visitors and how they respond to various experiences. Humans as a species instinctively pay greater attention to differences and changes in their environment. Any repetition will quickly lose visitor attention, and without attention it is difficult to create successful communication. Figure 2.2 shows the average time spent by visitors looking at paintings in art galleries, and it was initially described by Robinson in 1928 (cited in Bell et al., 1978). This pattern is one of the most common and enduring findings in visitor research. Robinson found the same pattern in four different art museums ranging in size from six rooms displaying 140 paintings to 40 rooms displaying more than 1,000 paintings. Figure 2.3 shows the results of two more recent Australian observation studies of visitor attention in settings with repetitive exhibits. These figures plot visitor responses to a series of nine dioramas in a cultural heritage center and a series of five backlit slides and text exhibits in an environmental interpretation center.

Looking at the reverse situation, equally clear and consistent patterns of results indicate the positive benefits of variety in interpretive activities. Numerous studies have been conducted which compare the traditional or common version of an interpretive activity, such as a trail or sign, with the same activity subjected to various alterations (see Moscardo, 1996a, for a more detailed review). Table 2.3 presents the results of a selection of these studies. There are three main points that can be made based on the patterns presented in Table 2.3. First, any interpretation is better than no interpretation. Second, interactive or participatory activities are often highly effective. The third and most significant conclusion that can be drawn, however, is that any change away from a traditional or expected format has the greatest impact on visitors.

Lew (1987) found that what visitors actually did at a holiday destination was often not well matched with what they wanted or expected to do. This study of visitors to Singapore further demonstrated that this mismatch was correlated with dissatisfaction with the travel experience. This story clearly warns us not to mistake quantity with quality. Lew's results also highlight the point that visitors to a region can only choose from the activities that are available. Tourism and recreation managers need to carefully consider the range and quality of the activities that they make available for their visitor. Destinations must provide a variety of activities from which guests can choose. Activities can be varied according to:
- where they are conducted (interpretive talks on a boat are very different from those given on a beach),
- when they are conducted (beach walks at night are very different from those conducted in the day),
- the level of physical effort required,
- the level of mental effort required (an interactive activity where visitors have to find answers to questions is a different experience from sitting, listening to a guide talk),

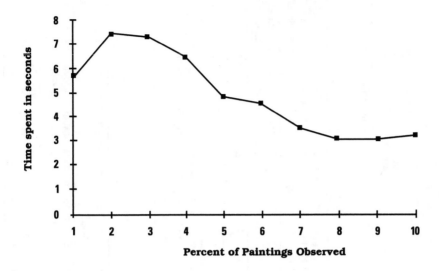

Figure 2.2: Basic pattern of visitor attention in art museums of varying sizes

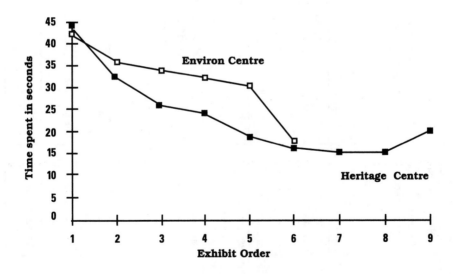

Figure 2.3: Patterns of visitor attention paid to repetitive exhibits

STUDY	SETTING	TYPES OF COMMUNICATION	MAJOR CONCLUSIONS
Birney (1988)*	Bird Area, Brookfield Zoo	Compared visitors looking at traditional cages of birds with those who participated in an interactive display on bird wing movement.	Visitors who participated were more knowledgeable than those who did not.
Bitgood et al. (1990)	African Plains Area at North Carolina Zoo	Visitors were observed before and after life-size cut-outs were placed on the boardwalk.	There was increased attention to the area after the cut-outs were introduced.
Blud (1990)*	An exhibit in London Science Museum	Compared a traditional display with text and illustrations to a push-button display and interactive display.	The interactive display created the greatest increase in visitor knowledge, but both the push-button and interactive versions were better than the static display.
Brockmeyer et al. (1983)*	Guided walk in a park in Columbus, Ohio	Visitors on a sensory walk (guide encouraged touch and smell) were compared to visitors taking a more traditional walk (just listening to guide and looking).	The sensory walk group remembered more about the walk than the other group.
Dowell & McCool (1986)	Missoula State Forest	Compared a slide show, booklet, and slide show with just the booklet.	All three approaches were better than nothing at all. Both slide show options were better than the booklet alone for increasing knowledge and creating positive attitudes towards management.
Falk et al. (1992)	California Museum of Science	Compared visitor responses to a traditional display and to a display where labels asked a question.	The new labels with the questions increased the time spent at the display and the amount of information visitors got from the display.
Horn (1980)*	Museum of Fine Arts, Boston	Two types of guided tours were compared. A traditional look-and-listen-to-the guide tour with an inquiry tour where the guide asks visitors questions and encourages discussion.	Much higher levels of enjoyment were reported by the visitors taking the inquiry tour.
Jacobson (1988)	Kinabula National Park, Malaysia	Compared a guided walk, a self-guided walk with a booklet, and a self-guided walk with signs along the trail to a walk on the trail with no interpretation.	All three types of communications were better than nothing at all. The guided walk was the best option. But the biggest increase in visitor knowledge was between nothing at all and adding the signs.
Korn (1988)	Japanese Garden, Chicago Botanical Garden	Studied visitors using a self-guided brochure with and without questions to those not using a brochure.	Both brochures improved visitor understanding.
Klevans (1990)*	Texas Memorial Museum	Evaluated visitors using an interactive computer exhibit.	Use of the computer resulted in significant increases in visitor knowledge.
Odgen et al. (1993)	Gorilla Tropics Area, San Diego Zoo	Added naturalistic sounds.	The use of natural sound increased visitor enjoyment and learning and had a positive influence on attitudes towards the animals.
Worts (1990)*	Art Gallery of Ontario	Compared visitors to a traditional gallery with visitors after interactive displays were installed.	The interactive displays were associated with increased attention to the art and greater enjoyment.

Table 2.3: Selection of studies into visitor responses to communication and interpretation

- who they are with, and
- the themes they pursue (a fishy, glass-bottom boat tour of a reef can be different from a tour of the same area which concentrates on corals and sponges).

These are just a few of the dimensions that can be varied to provide a range of interpretive activities. Individual activities also need to provide variety, and this can be done using many of the same dimensions listed above. A guide in charge of a forest tour can change the pace of the tour, ask questions instead of only answering them, focus the tour on different features of the forest, or focus on different members of the group. The guide could get the group to do things, touch things, smell things, as well as look at things. In short, using different senses, trying novel approaches, and providing surprises are all effective mechanisms for introducing variety into a tourist or recreation experience.

Interaction/Participation

Offering visitors an opportunity to participate directly in the communication or interpretation is both a way to provide variety and an important method for encouraging mindfulness. All those studies with an asterisk in Table 2.3 demonstrate the positive benefits of allowing visitors the opportunity to participate. It is important to note, however, that not all of what is seen by communicators as interactive is seen by visitors as interactive. Table 2.4 contains the results of a study conducted into the features of computer displays that contribute to their success. In particular, the study looked at the differences in visitor responses to computer exhibits with three levels of visitor participation (Moscardo, 1996b). The first level was a quiz game with a low level of participation. Visitors could only choose from a series of multiple-choice answers which were presented in a set order. The second level was an information program which allowed visitors to choose the topics and levels of information that the program gave them. The third level was a story game where the visitors could both personalize the story by playing the part of a character and control the program by choosing the topics, actions, order, and locations of the story components. The results presented in the table indicate that greater opportunity for visitor participation was usually associated with more positive outcomes.

OUTCOME	QUIZ GAME	INFORMATION PROGRAM	STORY PROGRAM
Time Spent (in minutes)	14	16	21
Enjoyment (0-10 scale)	6	7	8
Perceived Learning (0-10 scale)	8	10	9

Table 2.4: Results of an evaluation of different computer formats

In summary, it is important that communicators actually practice participation rather than just preach it, and that they recognize that participation involves giving some degree of control over the interpretation to the visitor. This may be as simple as a guide encouraging the visitors to ask questions and letting these questions direct the tour or talk a little, or as complex as a multimedia, virtual-reality experience that allows the visitors to create their own museum.

Personal Connections

Several of the studies summarized in Table 2.3 found that a guided tour or presentation was the most effective option. There are several possible explanations for this effectiveness of guides. It could be that they help visitors to find their way around, or that through their ability to answer questions, they can make the material presented personally relevant for visitors. Research describing guided tours in other settings emphasizes both these points (see Fine and Speer, 1985; Geva and Goldman, 1991; Pearce, 1984). An interesting variation of this feature was described by Diamond, Smith, and Bond (1988) where they observed that children were more likely to participate with exhibits in a Discovery Room when accompanied by an adult. In this instance, the authors pointed to the role of the adults in providing personal links to the objects displayed.

It is also clear from the comments made by visitors in survey and interview studies that being able to find or make a personal link is a major factor influencing their satisfaction and how much they feel they learn (see various studies by Wolf, Munley, and Tymitz).

In summary then, the Mindfulness Model, supported by evidence from visitors, gives us three important principles for encouraging mindfulness:
- providing variety,
- offering participation, and
- making personal connections.

One note of caution, however, must be made. While mindfulness is usually associated with various types of positive outcomes for visitors, it is not always automatically a pathway to improved learning and positive attitudes. It is a necessary, but not sufficient, condition for increasing knowledge and changing attitudes and behavior. The next section will consider some of the other features of communication situations which may influence outcomes.

A GENERAL MODEL OF COMMUNICATION

Much of our current understanding of communication is based on work conducted by social psychologists working at Yale University during the 1950s, 1960s, and 1970s. This group saw communication as having three main components, as set out in Figure 2.4. If we take this model and apply it to tourism and recreation settings, we would see the tourist operators and setting managers as the communicators, and the visitors as the audience. There are three important features of this model that must be pointed out.

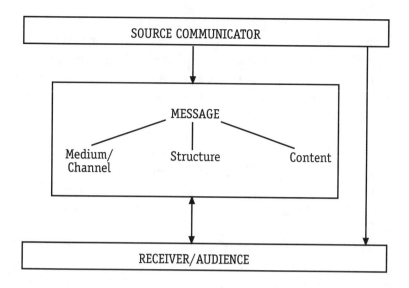

Figure 2.4: A basic model of communication

First, the message or the information to be communicated has three features. These are the actual content and how that content is organized and presented. The structure or organization of the message refers to such things as providing a list of facts versus telling a story, or asking questions versus providing a set of answers. The way it is presented (that is, the medium or channel) refers to such things as a brochure versus a guide presentation versus a sign versus a computer display. Many of the studies described in the previous section were examining these media or channels.

The second important feature of this model is that it has a double arrow connecting the message to the audience. The point of this double arrow is that it means that audiences or visitors are not passive receivers of information. People can actively choose to pay attention to some parts of a message and to ignore others. There is a group of researchers and communicators who have been concerned with better understanding the ways in which visitors change and use information according to how it fits what they already know or believe. A brief review of this work can provide some interesting information.

The clearest and most consistent finding from psychology research concerned with how people understand the world they live in is that we understand new information only when we can connect it to what we already know. We seek patterns in the world and give them meaning by comparing them to patterns that we already understand. These processes build complex systems of knowledge and understanding and help us make sense of the world (Kaplan and Kaplan, 1982; Miles, 1989; Wandersee, 1990).

If visitors construct meaning from the information presented by communicators and come to tourism and recreation situations with existing knowledge, then it is important for the communicators to understand the nature of this pre-existing knowledge. Borrowing from Pines and West's (1986) analysis, it is possible to suggest that there are three main relationships between an audience's pre-existing knowledge and the information and knowledge presented in interpretation. The first is one of conflict. In this situation, the construction or meaning of the communicator is very different from that held by the visitors. This is the situation most commonly examined in the literature on alternative or naive theories or misconceptions. There are numerous visitor studies which show that people misinterpret the meaning of exhibits and other forms of interpretation because they use a pre-existing theory which conflicts with the theory driving the interpretation (Miles, 1989; Pines and West, 1986). In this situation, it is often the case that visitors extract the information that makes sense to them, sometimes reinforcing the theory they brought with them (Miles, 1989).

In a second, similar situation, the visitors do not have enough knowledge of the topic to make sense of the information. This is especially true for many scientific topics such as gravity and evolution (Borun, 1991; Munson, 1994). Borun provides a good summary of this problem:

> *The first and most important thing we have to realize is that the majority of our visitors are novices—not experts. They lack the specialized knowledge base, language, concepts, and ways of thinking and looking which experts acquire through learning and practice. (1991, p. 4).*

In the third situation, the one most commonly assumed by communicators, the audience shares the same knowledge and background as the communicator. The evidence suggests that this is rarely the case. Wise communicators will seek to understand the meanings and constructions of knowledge visitors bring with them to tourism and recreation experiences.

The third important feature of the communication model presented in Figure 2.4 is that communicators can have a direct influence on the visitors. This is particularly true in guided situations where there is substantial and direct contact between the guide, or communicator, and the audience. This guide-visitor interaction is not always a successful one. One account of the interaction between guides and visitors in the Moremi Wildlife Reserve of Botswana noted a number of elements that contributed to a failed tourist experience (Almagor, 1985). In the first place, the guides and the visitors had very different goals for the experience. The visitors wanted to get as close as possible to the wildlife, while the guides saw their jobs as primarily keeping visitors safe and therefore away from the wildlife. The two groups also disagreed about the role of the guide. Visitors believed that guides should find wildlife, provide information about the wildlife, and serve as camping assistants. The guides believed that their job was to find the wildlife and make sure the visitors did not get lost or hurt. The interaction between the two groups was a failure because of these social problems.

If visitors do not like a guide or distrust a guide, then regardless of any other factors, communication will not work. The author has experienced and witnessed similar problems in several trips to Seal Bay National Park on Kangaroo Island, which lies off the South Australian coast. At Seal Bay, small groups of visitors are able to walk with a guide amongst a sea lion colony. Many of the guides provide excellent, interesting, and entertaining presentations about the sea lions and the park. I have, however, met some guides who were basically opposed to the idea of allowing visitors into the area. It is difficult as a visitor to be receptive to a message that begins with the lines:

You are not allowed to go closer to the sea lions than six meters. If you do, you will probably get bitten, and as far as I'm concerned, the more tourists who get bitten, the better.

PERSUASIVE COMMUNICATION

The results of research evaluating the performance of guides are consistent with results from research into persuasive communication. Persuasive communication research and theory specifically focuses on communication which has the aim of changing people's attitudes and behavior. Figure 2.5 outlines the various components of this field. This model suggests that there are several steps between communicating a message and changing visitor behavior. An effective communication must:

- get visitors' attention,
- be understood by visitors,
- be believed or accepted by visitors, and
- be remembered by visitors.

If it is to produce any change in visitors at all, an effective communication must also change visitors' beliefs or knowledge and their attitudes if it seeks to change their behavior.

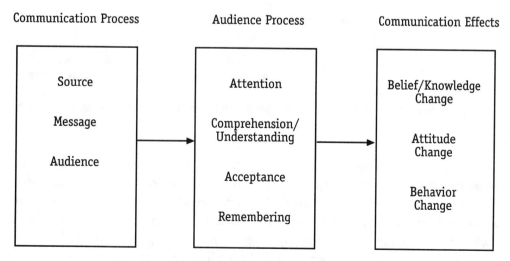

Figure 2.5: Major components of persuasive communication

(based on the model presented in Petty & Cacioppo, 1981)

COMPONENT	CONCLUSION
Communicators	Credible sources can be successful. Credibility comes from education, intelligence, and familiarity with the topic. Attractive communicators can be successful.
Features of messages	- Anecdotes are more successful than general abstract statistics. - Positive appeals are more effective than negative appeals. Negative appeals can be effective if they give detailed information and strategies to cope with the negative consequences portrayed. If a message has both positive and negative information, it is better to present the positive first. - A vivid example or information can be effective. Vividness is based on three features of information: emotional interest (the information/example relates to the individual or someone the individual knows), concreteness, and proximity to the individual (close in time or space). - Unexpected or contradictory information is remembered better than expected or consistent information. - Use of analogies, similes, and metaphors are effective in producing attitude change. - Explicit conclusions should be given. - It is better to acknowledge and refute opposing arguments early in the presentation than to ignore them. - It is better to leave out weak arguments. - It is preferable to state the basic position of the message at the beginning. - Repetition of arguments (if varied in presentation) is effective in increasing memory for the content and sustaining attitude change. - Informative messages are best; that is, the message gives detailed information on when, where, and what the receiver should do. The information should also be related to information that the receiver already has. - Direct experience or contact with an object/issue is successful in changing attitudes.

Based on reviews by Ajzen (1992); McGuire (1985); Fazio et al. (1983); Petty et al. (1992); and Sherer and Rogers (1984).

Table 2.5: Major findings from persuasive communications research

There has been research conducted into the various components and processes of persuasive communication, and some of the major findings are provided in Table 2.5. The most important findings, however, are those that suggest there are two different types of attitude change related to two different types of thinking. Two sets of researchers have been responsible for describing these two pathways to attitude change, Petty and Cacioppo (1986) and Chaiken and Stangor (1987). These researchers propose that one route to attitude change focuses on the context of a persuasive communication (called *heuristic processing* by Chaiken and Stangor, and *peripheral routes* by Petty and Cacioppo). The other concentrates on the content of the message (called *systematic processing* by Chaiken and Stangor, and *central routes* by Petty and Cacioppo).

In the first case, for example, the individual is persuaded by the expertise, authority, or credibility of the communicator and does not process the information in the message. This sort of response is associated with temporary attitude change and is unlikely to result in behavior change. The alternative is a central route or systematic processing, where the individual's attention is focused on the content of the message. There is a clear parallel here to Langer's mindfulness and mindlessness (Palmerino et al., 1984). As we might expect, the conditions that have been found to encourage central or systematic processing are the same as those which support mindfulness. (See Petty et al., 1992, for further discussion of this material.)

Summary

The review of models of communication and theories of persuasive communication has provided more support for the mindfulness model. The review has also suggested some additional information to consider. In particular, the review suggests that the structure of the message can greatly influence how easily it is understood. Visitor understanding is also affected by what visitors already know. Effective communicators, then, must know something about what their audience knows and think carefully about how they structure their message.

SOME THOUGHTS FROM VISITORS

I have previously used comments from visitors to support the Mindfulness Model. But what else can we learn from surveys and interviews with visitors? In a study conducted at the Hall of Human Biology at the British Museum of Natural History, Alt and Shaw (1984) asked visitors to generate lists of characteristics of

(In order from most to least important)

1. It arouses interest in the subject.
2. The information is clearly presented.
3. It teaches something new.
4. You can't help noticing it.
5. It gets the message across quickly.
6. It involves the visitor.
7. The visitors can take it at their own pace.
8. It's a memorable exhibit.
9. It respects the intelligence of the visitor.
10. It uses familiar things or experiences to make the point.

From Alt & Shaw (1984)

Table 2.6: Ten most important attributes of an ideal exhibit

exhibits and then to decide which of these characteristics were applicable to their ideal exhibit. Table 2.6 lists the top 10 ideal characteristics. Many of these characteristics are as would be expected. Visitors seek exhibits that catch their attention, that interest them, that make personal connections, and that are easy to follow. Of particular interest in this table is the visitor preference for communication that respects their intelligence.

A research program conducted at the various museums which form the Smithsonian Institution also provides results consistent with the Mindfulness Model (Cave and Wolf, 1983; Wolf, Munley, and Tymitz, 1979; Wolf and Tymitz, 1978, 1979). These researchers engaged in what they refer to as *naturalistic evaluation*. This involves participant observation of, and unstructured interviews with, groups of visitors. In a 1978 study of the Ice Age Mammals and Emergence of Man Exhibit, Wolf and Tymitz noted that visitors enjoyed exhibits which provided information relevant to their own experience and that

> *many visitors noted their interest in the Ice Age was partly stimulated by the severe weather conditions that had been occurring in the months during which the study was conducted. (p. 19)*

In a similar vein, a study of Discovery Corners in the National Museum of History and Technology found that the features visitors most liked about the corners were the opportunity to get information relevant to their own personal concerns, the opportunity to touch objects, and that the corners were different from the usual activities available in the museum (Wolf, Munley, and Tymitz, 1979).

Another common theme in these visitor comments was the need for physical orientation. A survey of visitors to the Anniston Museum of Natural History (Alabama) also found that orientation was important, for it was the most common improvement suggested by visitors (Bitgood et al., 1986). In a study which asked people to describe a visit to a museum, the biggest difference found between people who had never visited a museum and people who had was a concern with maps and finding one's way around (Moscardo, 1991). Very few people who have never been to a museum think about maps, visit plans, or getting to the exhibits. As experience increases, there is a consistent increase in the importance of this aspect of a museum visit.

Two major points emerge from this set of findings. The first is the need to respect visitors. Tilden, who wrote extensively about communicating with visitors to national parks, particularly stressed this point. Specifically, he quotes another communicator (Clark Wissler) as saying that

> *every ranger has the tendency to overestimate the background the tourist brings to the scene and on the other hand to underestimate the intelligence of the "average visitor." (1977, p. 46)*

The second important point is that visitors need help to find their way around in many tourist and recreation settings.

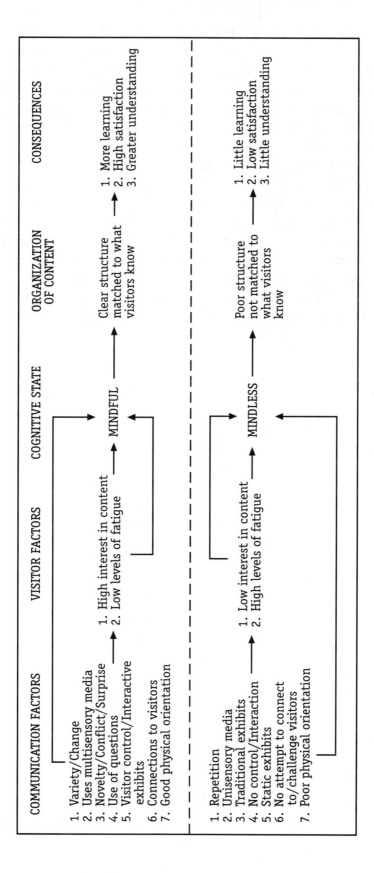

Figure 2.6: Mindfulness model for communicating with visitors

PRINCIPLES FOR ENCOURAGING MINDFUL VISITORS

In our review of what is already known about communication in tourist and recreation settings, we can see that there are some consistent patterns. Figure 2.6 provides a revised model to follow. From this model we can set out five principles for encouraging mindfulness and communicating effectively with visitors.

1. Help visitors find their way around.
2. Make connections to visitors and get them involved.
3. Provide variety.
4. Tell a good story that makes sense.
5. Know and respect visitors.

Now we know how to recognize a mindful visitor, and we have spent some time learning from other travelers (researchers who have studied mindfulness/mindlessness and communication). So we have an idea about what to expect. We can now start searching for more detail, and we can see how others have used the principles to create effective communication.

■ 3
Helping Visitors Find Their Way Around

> *You have taught me the fear of becoming lost, which has*
> *killed the pleasure of curiosity and discovery.*
> *(Keillor, 1985, p. 254)*

ALL TRAVELERS NEED good maps, and one important task for explorers is to make good maps of the new territories they find.

CHAPTER 3: OVERVIEW

AIMS	MAJOR THEMES	SECTIONS WILL PROVIDE
1. To demonstrate the importance of effective orientation systems.	**Getting lost distracts visitor attention and is a negative experience.**	Evidence that getting lost is both a common visitor experience and a negative experience.
2. To review research into cognitive mapping and map use.	**Good orientation systems provide support for communication.**	A review of the elements that can be used in an orientation system. A review of cognitive mapping research.
3. To derive some ideas for designing good orientation systems and better maps.	**We can develop good orientation systems and design better maps from understanding how people learn to find their way around in new places and how they respond to different types of maps.**	A review of studies into map use. Ideas for designing places in which it is easier to get around. A set of ideas.

BEING LOST IS NOT GOOD

Tourist and recreation settings are often complex and unfamiliar places, and getting lost is a common tourist experience (Walmsley and Jenkins, 1991; Pearce, 1982b). Having trouble finding your way around is costly in terms of time and effort and can be a very stressful experience (O'Neill, 1991). Many people have said that being lost is one of the most distressing experiences people can have (Lynch, 1960; Shumaker and Reizenstein, 1982; Black and Pearce, 1995; Kitchin, 1994). According to Zimring (1982), being disoriented makes people feel anxious, panicky, angry, frustrated, stressed, confused, and incompetent. If we do not help visitors find their way around, we will not be making them feel comfortable. We also risk simply not getting them. If they cannot find us, they cannot listen to us.

> *Many tourists arrive at their destination with vague to nonexistent cognitive maps of its environmental construction, content, pathways, and borders. To take advantage of available tourist attractions, entertainment, [interpretation] and retail facilities, these visitors must engage in some minimal level of environmental learning. To the extent that this level of learning can be increased or maximized, the degree of tourist interactions and consumption should also be increased or maximized.*
> *(Guy et al., 1990, p. 420)*

In other words, people need to have access to good orientation systems if they are to make effective use of the services being offered (Rovine and Weisman, 1989). Cohen (1977), for example, found that in a museum without orientation devices, 71 percent of visitors were unaware of the existence of entire halls or galleries, 86 percent had no idea what was the nearest hall, and 41 percent had been forced to backtrack at some point in their visit. In another study, visitors at a zoo who used a map were compared to visitors not given a map. The visitors with the maps went to more areas in the zoo than those who did not have a map and reported that the map was very useful in helping them to decide what to do (Bitgood and Richardson, 1987). Talbot et al. (1993) found higher levels of satisfaction reported by museum visitors who were given a map when compared to visitors not able to access a map. Good orientation can make a significant contribution to visitor satisfaction.

Good orientation can also contribute to visitor learning. If visitors are concentrating on finding their way around, then they will find it difficult to be mindful about any other communication. Several studies have demonstrated that people in new and unfamiliar settings spend a lot of energy on getting oriented and consistently learn less information than people who are familiar with a place (see Orion and Hofstein, 1994, and Falk, 1991, for a review of this work).

A simple exercise can help to demonstrate these points. Look at the map in Figure 3.1 and try to complete the following exercises:

1. Your location is given by the "X" in this map of an old, gold mining town. Plot the most efficient pathway through the area that will give you maximum exposure to the different buildings listed.

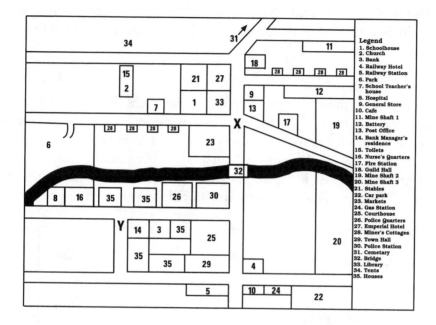

Figure 3.1: A map of Crowtown

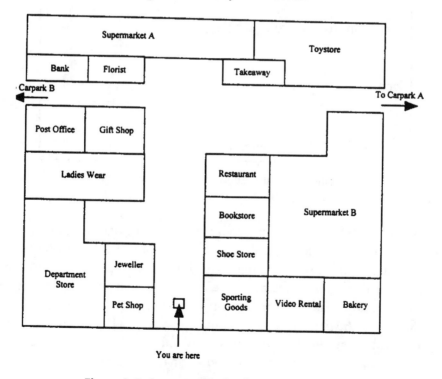

Figure 3.2: An example of a "you-are-here" sign

2. Where are the nearest bathrooms, and how quickly do you think you can get there?
3. How long do you think it would take you to get from where you are to point "Y"? And what do you think you will see when you get there?

This map is of a fictitious place and so there are no right or wrong answers. But the notes at the end of the chapter should help you think about some of the problems visitors can face.

What Are the Options?

What sorts of things can we do in tourist and recreation settings to help visitors find their way around? The most common option is a map that visitors can take with them as they move around an area. Another common device is putting maps on signs. Often these signs use "you-are-here" maps (see Figure 3.2). Directional signs such as those in Figure 3.3 are another orientation device that can be used, and it is also possible to have information desks with staff to give directions.

Park Headquarters (50 yards)	▶
Toilets (50 yards)	▶
Short Rainforest Walk (1 mile)	▲
Picnic Area (1/2 mile)	▲
Waterfall Lookout (2 miles)	◀

Figure 3.3: An example of a directional sign

Several studies in museums and zoos have asked visitors which of the previous options they prefer, and some results are given in Table 3.1. Maps (either hand-held or on signs) and directional signs are clearly preferred over an information desk. Despite the lower preferences given for hand-held maps in the studies in Table 3.1, there is evidence that many more visitors actually use them. Cohen et al. (1977) found that 60 percent of visitors, and Talbot et al. (1993) found 58 per cent of visitors used a hand-held map if one was available. Clearly, maps, either hand-held or on signs, are a dominant orientation or pathfinding device.

MAKING BETTER MAPS

Before discussing ways to make maps which visitors can use, it is worth considering briefly what a map is and some of the critical processes involved in map creation and map use. Firstly, it is important to recognize that a map is not a reproduction of a place; it is an abstract representation of the mapmaker's perception of a place (Wandersee, 1990; McCleary, 1979; Liben and Downs, 1997). The following two quotes from cartography (the discipline of map design) textbooks express this argument well.

Device	Bitgood & Patterson (1987a)	Bitgood & Richardson (1987b)
Hand-held Map	20%	75%
Direction Signs	40%	20%
Wall Maps	24%	25%
Information Desk	12%	15%

Table 3.1: Visitor preferences for orientation devices

Maps are powerful tools, and have been for centuries because they allow us to see a world that is too large and too complex to be seen directly. The representational nature of maps, however, is often ignored—what we see when looking at a map is not the world, but an abstract representation.

(MacEachren, 1995, p. v)

Maps are graphic (not photographic) representations which, by their very nature, are selective and symbolic.

(Tyner, 1992, p. 13)

When cartographers design maps, they choose various features to include and they translate these selected features into symbols such as contour lines for elevation and dots for towns. In order to use a map for pathfinding, a map user has to be able to
- understand and locate the symbols and translate these symbols back into the reality of the place she is in,
- understand that the map does not include all the features of the place, and
- find the features she needs to help her get around.

Figure 3.4 provides an overview of the map design and use process. There are many points where problems can occur, and these are highlighted in the diagram. These problems are clearly recognized in discussions of map design and are usually accompanied by a call for map designers to think carefully about map users (Tyner,

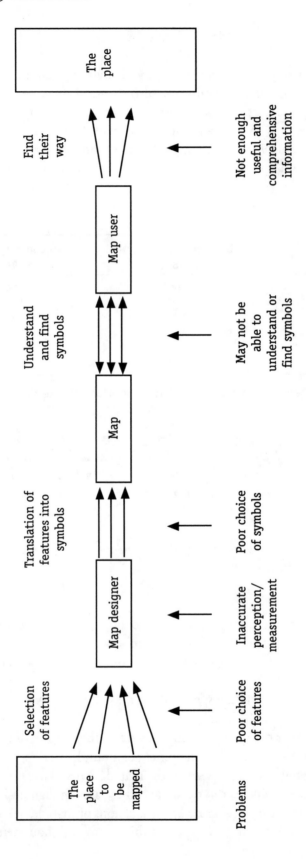

Figure 3.4: An overview of map design and use

1992; MacEachren, 1995; McCleary, 1979; Gerber, 1984; Liben and Downs, 1997). Unfortunately, it seems that map designers often become very concerned with their own conventions and traditions. The result is a widely held belief that many people have trouble using maps designed according to traditional cartographic conventions (Gerber, 1984; Keates, 1982; Spencer et al., 1989; Sholl, 1992; Talbot et al., 1993; Golledge et al., 1995).

How can we improve maps so that visitors can use them more easily and effectively to find their way around? There are two sets of information we can look at to get some answers to this question. The first area is research into how people actually find their way around in various places and how they store and use spatial information inside their heads. This field is called *cognitive mapping*. The second source of information is research into how people use different types of maps.

Cognitive Mapping

Cognitive mapping is the process of collecting, organizing, storing, remembering, and utilizing information about the surrounding environment.

(Guy et al, 1990, p. 421)

Cognitive mapping is a label used to describe the way we learn about spatial information and how we learn to get around in our environment (Glicksohn, 1994; Kitchin, 1994). Many psychologists believe that this process of cognitive mapping helps us to create and use cognitive or mental maps. They suggest that we can create maps in our heads and that we use these maps to help us find our way (Kitchin, 1994; Glicksohn, 1994; Walmsley and Jenkins, 1991; Gopal et al., 1989; Guy et al., 1990). Regardless of whether or not you believe we build maps in our heads, we can certainly all draw maps of places we have been, and these sketch maps can tell us interesting things about how people learn to get around.

The four maps in Figure 3.5 demonstrate some of the features that researchers have identified. The first map is my sketch map of where I work (I have studied or worked on this campus for about 15 years); the second was done by my eight-year-old son, who visits my office about 10 times a year. The third map was drawn by a visitor who has been to my office twice, and the fourth is my traced version of the official campus map. Before reading further, you might like to take a piece of paper and draw a map of your workplace.

My map (the map of a very experienced user) shows all five of the features consistently found in the maps people draw of familiar places. Firstly, you can see several **landmarks** are noted and highlighted—the swimming pool and the building with the eyelids. Landmarks are usually distinctive features which provide good reference points for navigation. My map also has many **paths** or routes for moving around the campus. In my map I have highlighted the major routes that I use to get around and made these stand out from the other possible routes. I have also identified **nodes** (which can be centers for activity or points where paths converge) such as the major road intersections and the student services center, and **districts** which are large areas with a common theme, such as the student residence area and the

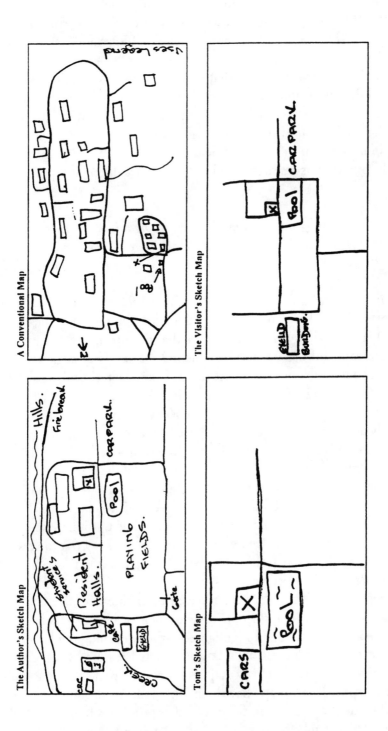

Figure 3.5: Sketch maps and conventional map of a university campus

sports field. Finally I have included some **edges** (the creek and the firebreak) which represent features that act as barriers to movement. All five of these features have been found in the maps people draw in studies conducted in many different places in the world (Lynch, 1960; Walmsley and Jenkins, 1991).

Landmarks

What else can we learn from these sketch maps in Figure 3.5? Look at the maps by the visitor and my son. They are both much simpler than mine and they both include only landmarks and paths. This is also a common finding in research. Children and new arrivals to an area seem to build up their knowledge of a place by first identifying and remembering distinctive features or landmarks and then learning a path or route as a sequence of landmarks. This is sometimes referred to as the "anchor point" theory. Landmarks are easy to remember and identify and so can be used as anchors for new information (Leiser and Zibershatz, 1989; O'Neill, 1991; Guy et al., 1990; Walmsley and Jenkins, 1991; Blades and Medlicott, 1992; Sholl, 1992; Tversky, 1992; Chown et al., 1995; Anooshian, 1996; Anooshian and Seibert, 1996). Looking again at all three sketch maps, we can see that the swimming pool and the eyelid building are major landmarks. These are both physically distinctive and located near an intersection. They are associated with an important point in a path where the person has to make a directional choice. Landmarks associated with choice points are especially useful and so are particularly important in cognitive or mental maps (Blades and Medlicott, 1992; Cornell et al., 1994).

Comparisons with Traditional Maps
Developing Detail

We can also derive some useful information by comparing the three sketches to the official map. The closest match to the official map is mine, the experienced-user map. My map has the most detail and includes many of the same features as the official map. This is what we would expect. As we develop more detailed knowledge about a place, our map of it becomes more and more like a traditional map with more accurate distances between places and more accurate directions (Anooshian, 1996; Walmsley and Jenkins, 1991). The maps of children and newcomers often either leave out angles such as turns or bends in paths or make them right angles (Glicksohn, 1994). Tom's map leaves out all the angles that are not associated with a decision, while the visitor's map uses all right angles.

Use of Compass Points

The official map is also presented so that the top of the map is aligned due north. None of the sketch maps uses cardinal or compass points, and it is usually the case that people do not use compass directions to find their way around (Blades and Medlicott, 1992). The two novice maps are both aligned so that my office (the core destination) is at the top. My map is aligned so that the entrances to the university are at the bottom and the mountains are at the top—a front-to-back alignment.

The two findings, that many map users do not use compass points or correct angles and directions, have led several map designers and researchers to suggest that stylized maps such as route maps might be more useful for users (Guy et al., 1990; Talbot et al., 1993; Holding, 1994; Monmonier, 1996; Kulhavy and Stock, 1996). Figure 3.6 provides an example of a stylized map.

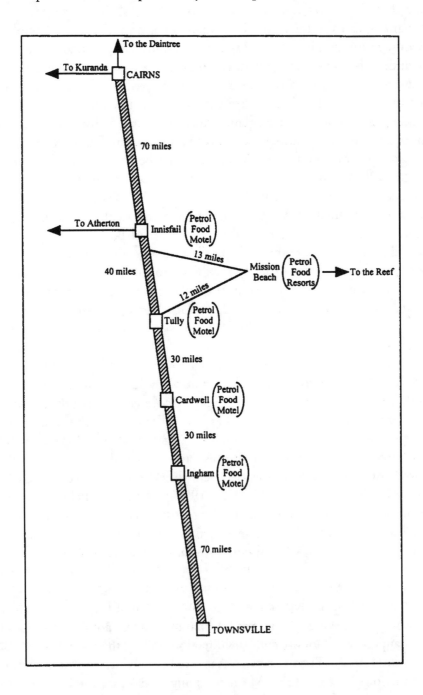

Figure 3.6: An example of a stylized map

Hierarchies of Information

The final key feature we can think about in the sketch maps is the way certain features are highlighted. In the official map, no particular features are highlighted. But in my map, several places are drawn in much larger than they are—particularly my office building, the library, the CRC Research building, and the cafe. These are the places that I both visit the most and see as important. This reflects a hierarchy of importance. I have also used a hierarchy in my roads. The ones I use the most are heavier—even though sometimes they are, in reality, smaller and narrower. This use of hierarchical organization of features is another common research finding (Tversky, 1992; Holding, 1994; Kitchin, 1996). A study of Parisian taxi drivers provides another example. These professional navigators learn a primary set of main roads and then fill in their maps with various other, secondary roads. When they have to get to a place, they use the first level of their hierarchy, the primary roads, to get as close as possible to the target, and then they use their knowledge of the secondary roads. They follow this plan in preference to plotting a course through the secondary roads (Leiser and Zibershatz, 1989).

Summary

Kitchin (1994) believes that it is possible to design better maps from an understanding of how people develop their own mental or cognitive maps.

Research Findings	Map Design Implications
1. Landmarks are critical reference points.	1. Maps should highlight distinctive and/or useful landmarks.
2. Paths/routes are the second step in learning about places.	2. Maps should highlight key paths or routes.
3. People do not use cardinal or compass points.	3. Align map to match use or the user's perspective.
4. People highlight and use important information.	4. Maps should highlight important or commonly used features.
5. Angles and directions are not as important as sequences.	5. Stylized maps such as strip maps should be useful.

Studies of Map Use

The second place we can find information to help us design better maps is in studies of how people respond to different types of maps. This is, unfortunately, an area where research has been scarce. Despite this, there are some patterns of results which can be used to develop better maps, and these are listed in Table 3.2. The two most commonly reported results, that highlighting key landmarks and aligning a map to the user's perspective are preferred, are consistent with what we know about cognitive mapping.

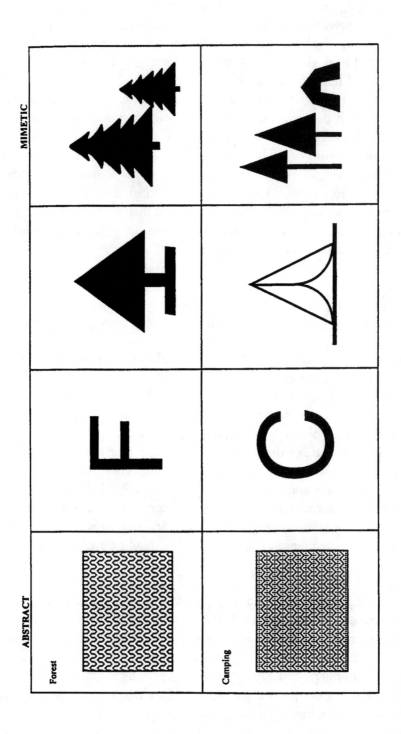

Figure 3.7: Types of symbols

Feature Found to Improve Map Use and Attractiveness	Studies
Including distinctive/highlighted landmarks	Devlin & Bernstein (1995) Warren (1994) Pearce & Black (1984)
Maps on signs should be aligned from the user's perspective	Levine (1982) Palij et al. (1984) Gopal et al. (1989) Glicksohn (1994)
Mimetic symbols (rather than abstract symbols)	Kulhavy & Stock (1996)
Text on the map (rather than beside it)	Kulhavy & Stock (1996)
Color codes	Garland et al. (1979) Gallagher (1983) Simutis & Barsam (1983)

Table 3.2: A summary of some research into maps

The finding with regard to the types of symbols used is also not unexpected if we think back to the diagram of the map design and use the models in Figure 3.4. The symbols chosen by map designers need to be easily understood by the map users (Keates, 1982; Monmonier, 1996; Tyner, 1992). Obviously, the more we can make a symbol look like the feature it represents, the easier it will be to understand. Mimetic symbols are those that look like (or mimic) the feature. Figure 3.7 shows a series of increasingly abstract symbols. The symbols on the right require less mental energy from the user than those on the left.

This idea of mental energy or effort is an important one in Black and Pearce's (1995) theory of cognitive steps and in Levine's (1982) concept of cognitive operations. These researchers believe that every translation or abstraction from reality that a map contains requires the user to expend mental effort. The more transformations in the map, the more cognitive steps the user has to take, the harder the map is to use. Pearce and Black put this hypothesis to the test, selecting real tourist maps which were three-dimensional, colored, and which had text on the map and pictures of landmarks (least steps). These were compared to two-dimensional, black-and-white maps with legends and no pictures (most steps). Their sample of users clearly preferred the maps with the least steps. Tests of map use, however, did not favor the least-steps maps. One of the problems was that in the sample of real maps, the least-steps maps were also the largest and tended to be maps of whole regions rather than single sites and so contained much more information. This need to keep maps simple is clear in two studies where visitors are asked to comment on varied map designs. Talbot et al. (1993), for example, found that visitors had a clear preference for simpler maps which contained less information. Lockett et al. (1989) found substantial support from visitors for adding pictograms, color, and additional place names. But this was only the case when the numbers of added features were not too great.

Summary

From this discussion of research into map use, the following principles for making effective maps can be outlined:
1. Use Highlighted/Three-dimensional/Pictures of key landmarks.
2. Use mimetic or less abstract symbols.
3. Align a map on a sign so that it matches the perspective of the user.
4. Put text on the map rather than numbers/letters and a legend.
5. Use color.
6. Be selective and moderate in your use of color, text, symbols, and land-marks. A simpler map will be a better map.

DESIGNING A COMPLETE STRATEGY

In the previous sections, we have concentrated our attention on maps. But what about other orientation devices such as directional signs? The studies of visitor preference reported in Table 3.1 suggested that some people prefer to use directional signs or information desks. Unfortunately, virtually no research has been published on the features of effective directional signs, information desk directions, or other devices such as colored lines to follow on the floor. There have been, however, a few studies comparing the effectiveness of maps with directional signs and maps with verbal directions. The results, though, have been variable. In two studies, few differences were found between the various devices examined (O'Neill, 1992; Kirasic and Mathes, 1990), while in others, directional signs were found to help people get to their destination faster than a "you-are-here" map (Butler et al., 1993; Kitchin et al., 1997). Cohen et al. (1977) found that people in museums use the different devices to achieve different goals. A hand-held or wall map can be used to get an overview of what is available and to make decisions about what to do and see, while directional signs help keep the visitors on their selected path. There is also some evidence from cognitive mapping research that people can and do change their orientation strategies to suit the conditions that they find (Spencer et al., 1989; Walmsley and Jenkins, 1991; Anooshian, 1996; Lawton, 1996; Anooshian and Seibert, 1996).

If people have varied preferences and different uses for different devices, then a wise tourism or recreation manager will create a complete orientation system using maps, hand-held and on signs, as well as directional signs and cues (Kitchin, 1994; Bitgood and Patterson, 1987b).

Designing the Setting as Well

A wise tourism or recreation manager can also think about building directional or orientation information into the places for which they are responsible. Bitgood et al. (1991), for example, observed museum visitors in galleries with and without island cases (displays in the center of pathways). They concluded that the islands created confusion and interrupted the flow of visitors. Their recommendations included removing the islands, using large and distinctive objects as landmarks for visitors, and numbering exhibits.

O'Neill (1991, 1992) and Lawton et al. (1996) have both noted that one of the major contributing factors to spatial confusion is the number of choice points or potential paths that exist in a setting. Figure 3.8 provides examples of a place with many and a place with few choice points. The greater the number of options, the more difficult it is for people to find their way. One solution is to close off some doors or paths to encourage a major route.

Other design options include the use of color or architectural design features to identify areas (Bitgood, 1987). In a zoo or a theme park, maps and actual spaces could be linked by the use of color. If a particular area is blue on the map, then blue could be the dominant color used in the signs, paths, or structures in that area.

Clearly, not every place is suitable for such interventions. But even in those tourism and recreation settings that cannot be changed, it is worth considering how well you make use of the distinctive features available in the design of orientation systems.

HOW YOU CAN HELP VISITORS FIND THEIR WAY AROUND

1. Think about the distinctive features and pathways available in a tourist or recreation setting. Can you make better use of the features that are available? Can you adapt your place so that paths are simpler and places are easier to recognize?
2. Develop a complete orientation system. Use a variety of devices (signs and maps) and think about how they complement each other. For example, do you use the same symbols on both your directional signs and your maps? Are color codes consistent across signs and maps? Are your signs and maps accurate?
3. Align any fixed maps so that they match the perspective of the visitors.
4. Design effective maps. This means:
   - Including important information (and excluding excessive detail).
   - Highlighting important landmarks and major paths or routes.
   - Using realistic symbols.
   - Putting text on the map instead of beside it.
   - Using some color if you can.

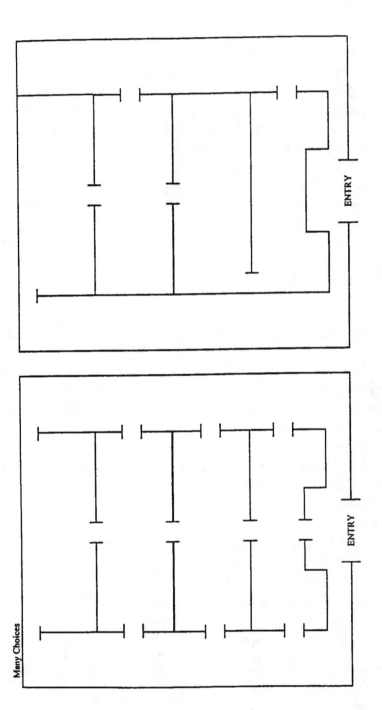

Figure 3.8: Reducing choice points and potential paths

Note: Finding Your Way around Crowtown

Crowtown (see p. 43, Figure 3.1) is an abandoned, turn-of-the-century, gold-mining town. Most of the buildings are gone, and only the Railway Hotel, fire station, and schoolhouse remain standing. The church, post office, and bank manager's residence are recognizable from the remaining walls and steps, everything else is gone. If you found the bathrooms on the map, well done. If not, they are behind the church ruins (building number 2). Getting there seems simple, but the map does not tell you that the church is on top of a hill and the walk up from point "X" is quite steep. Point "Y" is also on top of a hill, but the walk should only take you about five minutes, and when you get there, you will be able to see all of Crowtown!!

■ 4
Connecting to Visitors

ACCORDING TO VISITORS, the 10 most important features of a communication or interpretation activity are:

1. It arouses interest in the subject.
2. The information is clearly presented.
3. It teaches something new.
4. You can't help noticing it.
5. It gets the message across quickly.
6. It involves the visitor.
7. The visitor can take it at his own pace.
8. It is a memorable exhibit.
9. It respects the intelligence of the visitor.
10. It uses familiar things or experiences to make the point.

You may recognize these points from Chapter 2 (see Table 2.6). They are repeated here because they highlight several important points which will be covered in this chapter. In particular, this chapter will present ideas and examples for:

1. Getting visitor attention,
2. Getting visitors involved and giving visitors control, and
3. Making personal connections.

GETTING VISITOR ATTENTION

When we concentrate our senses and thinking upon some object, we are said to be paying attention to it. *Attention* is a basic concept in psychology, and there have been very many studies into what catches our attention. Several features of an object or a physical setting can automatically attract attention. These are:

1. *Extreme stimuli—very large, very colorful, very loud, and very smelly things—automatically attract attention.*
2. *Movement and contrast attract attention.*

3. *Unexpected, novel, and surprising things capture attention.*
4. *Other living things—people and animals—attract attention.*
5. *Things connected to us attract our attention.*

(Myers, 1986)

Table 4.1 provides several examples of how these general psychological principles can be translated into specific features of communication or interpretation activities. The examples are all taken from reports of research which has demonstrated that these features do work in attracting visitor attention. In addition to the features included in Table 4.1, a common visitor research finding is that interactive exhibits such as computers, microscopes, and objects that can be touched attract more visitor attention than static displays (Abrahamson et al., 1983; Koran et al., 1984; Diamond et al., 1988; Foster et al., 1988; Hilke et al., 1988; Worts, 1990). These interactive opportunities attract attention because they are often unexpected and offer a contrast to the displays around them.

The studies in Table 4.1 give us some ideas about how to use features such as size, color, movement, contrast, and interaction to attract visitor attention. More examples and ideas are always useful. The Head Smashed In Buffalo Jump Visitor Center in Alberta, Canada, uses a combination of size and surprise to capture visitor attention. Inside the entrance to this center, visitors are confronted by a replica of a cliff face and three buffalo which appear to be about to tumble over onto the visitors. The use of large red buffalo silhouettes draws visitors along a hallway to the start of the clifftop trail. This is a clever combination of orientation and attention getting. The visitor center in the World Heritage area of Cradle Mountain National Park (Tasmania, Australia) attracts visitors to enter with a wall-sized photograph of Cradle Mountain placed opposite the entrance door. This impressive

CHAPTER 4: OVERVIEW

AIMS	MAJOR THEMES	SECTIONS WILL PROVIDE
1. To review research and examples of effective ways of getting visitors involved, and making personal connections to visitors. 2. To provide a set of ideas for connecting to visitors.	**Effective communicators need to get and keep visitor attention.** **The best way to get and keep visitor attention is to get them to participate in the experience, and to make information personally relevant or important.** **Giving visitors choices and control is a good way to get visitors involved.**	Ideas for getting visitor attention. Ideas for getting visitors involved and giving them control. Ideas for making personal connections to visitors.

PRINCIPAL	EXAMPLE	STUDY
Extreme Stimuli	1. Several studies have found that visitors are attracted by larger animals.	Bitgood et al. (1988) Foster et al. (1988)
	2. In aquaria/marine parks, visitor attention is more easily attracted by large tanks.	Serrell (1977) Moscardo (1993a)
	3. Large paintings/illustrations attract attention.	Bitgood (1988)
	4. Large objects in general attract attention.	Bitgood et al. (1991) Korenic (1991)
	5. Colorful objects attract attention.	Korenic (1991)
	6. Color added to signs attracts greater visitor attention.	Arndt et al. (1992)
	7. Larger type on signs attracts attention.	Thompson & Bitgood (1988)
	8. Adding sound to a display increases attention.	Wolf & Smith (1993) Peart (1984)
Movement & Contrast	1. Moving objects such as models/machinery attract visitor attention.	Melton (1936) Pearce (1988)
	2. Active animals attract more attention.	Bitgood et al. (1988)
	3. Contrast on signs or labels attracts attention.	Wolf & Smith (1993)
Unexpected, novel, surprising things	1. Unusual plants in terms of shape or color attract more attention.	Korenic (1991)
	2. Animal silhouettes on a nature trail attract more attention.	Bitgood et al. (1990)
	3. Multisensory displays attract more attention.	Davidson et al. (1991)
	4. Provocative headings on signs attract attention.	Kanel & Tamir (1991) Rand (1985)
Living things	1. Live animals attract more attention than other displays.	Moscardo (1993a) Serrell (1977)
Personal Interest	1. Greater interest in a topic has been related to greater attention paid to a topic.	Koran et al. (1989) Bechtel (1967)

Table 4.1: Features that attract visitor attention

visual aid not only draws people into the center but also across to that side of the center where visitors find the entrance to a rainforest boardwalk.

Museums, visitor centers, and theme parks can easily incorporate many of these features (particularly size) into their design to attract people into and through displays and galleries. Guided tours or presentations require a little more thought. Table 4.2 presents several different possible introductions for a guided tour to demonstrate some of the ways a guide or presenter can focus visitor attention on her tour or presentation. The first is the traditional and very common introduction. Clearly, the information is important and should be given to visitors early on in the tour, but it is not as interesting and as attention grabbing as the other approaches. The second uses an unusual object and poses a question to get visitor attention, while the third uses sound to focus visitors on the tour and the fourth sets up a challenge for visitors. After getting attention, we can then give visitors the necessary information about the tour.

We can apply the same principles to get visitors to begin to read signs and brochures. We know from Table 4.1 that color, contrast, larger type, and larger size all enhance a sign's ability to attract visitor attention. Rand (1985) suggests the use

---

1. Good evening, my name is Cathy and I will be your guide on our beach walk this evening. I've worked here with the resort as an interpretive officer for two years and so I know this beach very well. Our tour will last about two hours, and during that time we will have walked right around the island, which is a distance of about 4 miles. If you have any questions as we go along, please ask.

2. Hello, everyone, my name is Cathy and I'd like you all to have a look at this object or thing that I'm holding. We can pass it around and touch and smell it. It's something we will see several times in our walk this evening and I wonder if anyone can tell what it is and where it might have come from? (Object is a mangrove seed washed onto the island from the mainland.)

3. Hello, everyone, my name is Cathy and I'd like you to listen to this tape of some island sounds for a minute. (Plays tape.) That's a pretty eerie sound, and you can understand why the early settlers here thought the island was haunted. It is actually the sound of a small bird that nests on the island, and if we're not too loud, we will probably see some on our walk tonight.

4. Hello, everyone, my name is Cathy and our walk this evening is going to take us right around the island. Along the way, we will be seeing a lot of seaweed. We should be able to see at least 15 different types of seaweed. I'm going to give everyone a recording chart and a pencil and we're going to try and identify all 15. If we do well, the resort chef has said we can all come back for seconds for dessert at dinner tonight.

**Table 4.2: Examples of guided tour introductions
(An evening beach walk on an island)**

1. Provocative

        Squids have orgies, but octopuses have close encounters.

        Another mystery of the deep.

2. Challenging

        They may look empty, but mudflats crawl with life.

        This plant-like creature is actually an animal.

3. Ask Questions

        Which jaws could crush a crab?

        Can you find the flat fishes?

From Rand, 1985

Table 4.3: Some examples of sign titles to attract attention

of provocative statements, challenges, and questions in sign titles to attract attention. Table 4.3 contains some examples of such titles.

These examples are all about getting or attracting visitor attention. But what about holding or keeping that attention? Table 4.4 contains the results of two Australian visitor observation studies conducted by the author. One study involved observing the behavior of more than 1,200 visitors to an aquarium and marine center in a tourist complex (the Great Barrier Reef Aquarium in the Great Barrier Reef Wonderland in Townsville), while the other was conducted at the Skyrail Rainforest Cableway attraction in Cairns, where more than 950 visitors were observed. The results in the table are organized in two categories:

1. High success at **both** attracting and keeping visitor attention, and
2. High success at attracting but not keeping attention.

The results from these two studies tell us that extreme stimuli, such as size, color, and movement, can attract or get visitor attention but, on their own, are unlikely to keep visitor attention. **Interactive** options, however, seem to be successful at both attracting and keeping visitors.

GETTING VISITORS INVOLVED AND GIVING THEM CONTROL

Many authors, communicators, and teachers have argued for the need to get people to participate in activities rather than just listen to or read information. The need to get interactive and participatory has become such a well-established rule that hardly anyone even talks about it anymore. But what makes a communication or interpretation program truly participatory? The mindfulness model would argue that choice and control are the two factors that can move an activity from hands on to minds on.

In both the previous section of this chapter and parts of Chapter 2, we found that even small and simple activities such as allowing visitors to touch and handle things and adding sound to displays and tours can significantly increase visitor

CATEGORY	AQUARIUM EXHIBITS	RAINFOREST ACTIVITIES
1. Exhibits/Attractions/ Activities which **attract** and **keep** visitor attention.	A **large** touch tank which has **moving, living** animals that visitors can **touch**. Three **large** (10 square feet) windows into a huge reef tank where visitors can see many **colorful, active** fish and other marine life. Two **large** windows into a predator tank full of **large** turtles and sharks. A **discovery** room where people can **use microscopes** to examine objects (**choice**).	A lookout over a set of waterfalls into a rainforest gorge (**size & movement**). An **interactive** computer display which allows people to hear the **sounds** of rainforest animals that the visitors **choose**. A rainforest video (**multi-sensory**). An **interactive** computer quiz. Two **touch** tables where visitors can handle seeds and objects (**choice**).
2. Exhibits/Attractions/ Activities which **attract** attention but don't keep it. (That is, people stop but don't stay).	Set of **large, colorful** backlit slides of coral reefs. Four small tanks containing a variety of fish (**living creatures**).	Two lookouts over the rainforest gorge (not the waterfalls and usually visited after the main falls lookout) (**size**). Traditional static display on rainforest diversity (**adjacent** to computer displays). Sign near a **large** tree.

Table 4.4: Attracting and holding visitor attention

attention. The core feature of these options is that they change the experience from being focused on one sense (usually sight) to allowing visitors to use several senses (such as smell, sound, and touch). Having information from several senses does encourage us to be more mindful.

There is plenty of evidence, however, that we can encourage further mindfulness by moving from things such as touch tables to more interactive options. Before getting into some examples of how we can make our communication with visitors more interactive, it is worth considering what we mean when we use the terms *interactive* or *participatory*. There has been some debate about when an activity offered to visitors can truly be seen as participatory. Some authors have argued that truly participatory communication allows the visitors to influence or change the information that they get (Miles et al., 1982). Thus, on a tour, having the guide ask visitors questions would not be as participatory as getting visitors to ask the guide questions. In a visitor center, pushing buttons to start a model working or lifting flaps to find an answer to a question are not truly interactive activities. But the evidence suggests that it is usually better to have these activities than to have a static or passive option.

Koran et al. (1983a) have suggested that instead of a dichotomy where something is or is not participatory, it is better to think about participation as a continuum running from none at all through to a great deal. Figure 4.1 demonstrates this continuum for an exhibit or display. Each step along the continuum adds another sense, another physical activity, or another mental activity. Each step also allows the visitor to have a greater impact on the activity.

Table 4.5 contains text taken from four signs in national parks in North Queensland, Australia. These signs are examples of how we can encourage participation from visitors. In a similar way, guided tours and presentations can encourage visitor participation. A guide or presenter can

- ask visitors questions about the content,

No Participation Unisensory No control	1. Traditional display of shells with labels in a case. (Look & Read Only)
Add to senses	2. Change to a diorama or replica of a beach with the shells displayed *in situ* and with marine sounds.
Add to senses Some choice over what to touch	3. Add a touch table with shells that can be handled.
More control Greater physical activity	4. Add a microscope/magnifying glass so visitors can look at shells in more detail.
More control	5. Add an option for visitors to read from various books on shells.
Full Participation Multisensory Full control	6. Add a computer program which allows visitors to choose different types of shells or places where shells are found. The computer provides audiovisual presentations and personalized information printouts.

Figure 4.1: A participation continuum for exhibits/displays
(Based on Koran et al., 1983a)

1. Ask a question and encourage mental activity.

   From rainforest to sea
   You have just left the rainforest and are entering the mangroves. How do the two forests differ? Well, for one thing, mangroves love wet feet. The trees have adapted to living "between the tides."
   (From Marrdja Boardwalk, QNPWS)

2. Suggest activities.

   Not every bit of the Wet Tropics is rainforest. In some places the rainforest flashes in and out of sight like the sparkle of a precious stone. Hidden amongst the gum trees of Jourama Falls are jewels of moist, green rainforest in the Wet Tropics' crown.

   Walk to the lookout. Search the hill slopes for dark green patches, the moist valleys where rainforest hides.

   Walk along Waterview Creek. Explore the shady rainforest bordering the creek.

   Stand at the Lookout. Look up to the mountains, capped in dark green. Rainforest thrives at higher altitudes.
   (From Jourama Falls Sign, WTMA)

3. Suggest actions visitors can take. (This section follows other information on cassowaries.)

   How can you help?

   As a visitor to Mission Beach, you can help in cassowary conservation.

   • **Do not feed cassowaries**

   Feeding can introduce disease and can increase cassowary fatalities through association of food with humans and vehicles. It can also be dangerous, as a hungry cassowary can become aggressive towards humans. Be sure to secure all rubbish bins.

   • **Reduce vehicle speed**

   When traveling through cassowary country, travel slowly. Remember cassowaries need to cross roads in search of food.
   (From Tam O'Shanter State Forest)

QNPWS - Queensland National Parks and Wildlife Service
WTMA - Wet Tropics Management Authority

Table 4.5: Some examples of signs which encourage participation

- get visitors to ask questions,
- get visitors to touch, smell, and taste things,
- set up quizzes or puzzles for visitors to solve,
- get visitors to play various roles, and
- seek topics of interest to the visitors and use these to shape the content of the tour or presentation.

In each of these examples, increasing participation allows for greater visitor control. In Chapter 2, I reported the results of a study into visitor responses to different types of computer programs. In that study I showed that people spent longer time, learned more, and had greater enjoyment from a program that allowed them to choose the topics, actions, order, and locations in a story. In this study, a quiz game with a set order of questions gained the lowest scores for enjoyment, learning, and time spent; better results came from greater opportunities to be in control (Moscardo, 1996b). This study was developed from an earlier study which examined how visitors behaved at six computer displays in four different settings: a maritime museum, a museum of natural history, and two historic buildings. Three of the computers offered quiz-type games and used sound and graphics to enhance the experience, while the other three were information programs. One allowed visitors to trace the history of the suburb where they lived; another one provided information on the migration patterns of different ethnic or cultural groups; and the third allowed visitors to enter their surname and get related historical information. None of these programs used sound or graphics, and all of them required some effort to understand and use. But the observations showed that visitors spent more time at the information programs and were more likely to wait and participate than visitors observed at the quiz programs (see Table 4.6 for the details results). The common feature shared by the three successful programs was that visitors had control over the information they accessed and they could use this control to find information that was personally relevant (Moscardo, 1989).

In general, feeling in control of a situation is a good thing. It can increase our self-esteem and help us feel happy. Giving visitors some control in tourism and recreation settings not only can make them feel good, it can also help communicators make various communication activities, such as guided tours, more participatory. If we think about control as the key feature, we can think about simple options rather than high-technology-based activities. Many of the examples of interactive communication used both here and in other texts involve displays and expensive technology such as computers. The key point to remember, though, is that what works best is control. One of the cheapest displays I have seen was a pinboard

VARIABLES	INFORMATION PROGRAMS	QUIZ PROGRAMS
Mean Time Spent at the display	3 minutes 41 seconds	1 minute 57 seconds
% look at screen only	5%	10%
% watch others participate only	30%	57%
% wait & then participate	12%	4%
% participate	23%	11%

From Moscardo (1989)

Table 4.6: Results of computer display study

with recycled notepaper and a basket of pencils. Visitors were asked to write down a short story about a sea voyage they had experienced. The result was an exhibit which was virtually created by the visitors, constantly changing and very popular. When visitors can make choices about the information they access, they can also create unique and personal experiences. The mindfulness model tells us that personal relevance is a critical element in successful communication.

MAKING PERSONAL CONNECTIONS

Many of the readers who have backgrounds in dealing with visitors to national and state parks and forests will be familiar with the writing of Freeman Tilden. Tilden first wrote about interpreting to visitors in 1957, and he set out a series of principles for good interpretation. The first of these was that

> *Any interpretation that does not somehow relate what is being displayed or described to something within the personality or experience of the visitor will be sterile.*
>
> *(1977, p. 9)*

Tilden's argument was that we need to make personal connections. He goes on to provide a simple example of how such connections can be made when he reports on an exhibit label in a museum in Texas. The label read:

> *"Prehistoric mammoths were here in Texas just a few thousand years ago. They roamed the plains in great herds ... The chances are that they browsed right where **you** are standing **now**." Where **you** are standing **now**. With that statement the mammoths are not far away creatures of time or space but right under your feet.*
>
> *(1977, pp. 13-14)*

One of the simplest approaches to making a connection is using a conversational style in signs and text, and this is recommended by many authors (Volkert, 1991; McManus, 1989; Rand, 1985). Figure 4.2 has two versions of a sign. The first is an actual sign, while the second version takes virtually the same text and presents it in a direct, conversational style. When asked to compare the two, 97 percent of people preferred the second.

Clues to other ways to make personal connections can be found in the comments visitors themselves make. Table 4.7 provides a small sample of some visitor comments. Some of the options described by the visitors include:

1. **Using analogies and metaphors that link the interpretive content to the everyday experience of the visitor.** Wurman (1989) gives us several good examples of using comparisons to everyday objects and familiar experiences.

The analogies the woman used were ones that any child could understand. It was really great (Wolf, Munley, & Tymitz, 1979, p. 32).

You really learn more if there is a story or an experience. You can look all day, but if it all comes closer to home, you remember more if you can come closer to the objects (Wolf, Munley, & Tymitz, 1979, p. 29).

Having a person to ask questions was really good. The woman can talk and answer the questions that we have—an exhibit can't (Wolf, Munley, & Tymitz, 1979, p. 33).

You can handle the objects, touch them and feel them. You're not just looking in, but you can be part of it too (Wolf, Munley, & Tymitz, 1979, p. 34).

Putting Snoopy in there shows the museum has a sense of humor. I like that ... Everything doesn't have to be dry and scientific. Having Snoopy there shows that the museum is part of our daily life (Wolf & Tymitz, 1981, p. 32).

I'd like to learn about ways to improve the environment. There should be more about the future—what's going to happen, what we can do (Wolf & Tymitz, 1981, p. 39).

When I go through the hall on the rocks, I see lots of rocks placed by other rocks and I see the categories and classifications of rocks—but in here if I don't want to look at the fossils, I can choose to look at other kinds of things that the museum has. I guess what I'm saying is I feel like I have a choice (Wolf & Tymitz, 1981, p. 19).

Table 4.7: Visitor comments on personal connections and relevance

Facts are only meaningful when they relate to a concept that you can grasp. If I say an acre is 43,560 square feet, that is factual but it doesn't tell you what an acre is. On the other hand, if I tell you that an acre is about the size of an American football field without the end zones, it is not as accurate, but I have made it understandable.

(pp. 172-173)

2. **Telling stories with characters that visitors can relate to.** One of the options suggested for self-guided tours around a historic village was to develop a series of brochures, each connected to a particular character. The brochure would then help guide the visitor through the village, taking a path that the character might have taken, and present the various sites through the eyes of the character. The series could include a child, a schoolteacher, a clerical worker, a railway worker's wife, a policeman, and a miner. It would cover both males and females and people varying in age. The visitors could choose the character most like themselves or in whom they were most interested (Moscardo et al., 1995).

3. **Choosing and presenting topics and contents directly related to visitor experiences.** Tilden (1977) provides an example of this when he tells a story about presenting the pottery of a pre-Columbian culture. According to Tilden, it is better to present aspects of the daily lives of the people than details of the changing shapes and colors used in the pottery. Webb and Wotton (1993) provide another example of choosing topics relating to the

ORIGINAL VERSION

The Stinging Tree

Although the serrated, heart-shaped leaves and fleshy red berries of the stinging tree often remind people of a raspberry bush, don't be tempted. Stay well clear!

Found primarily in the rainforest, the stinging tree has a dense covering of fine, glass-like hairs on all exposed parts of the plant. If accidentally brushed against, the hairs break off and lodge in the skin. These hairs release a chemical which can cause a throbbing pain that can last many months.

Historical records show that animals are equally susceptible to the virulent poison produced by the hollow hairs of the stinging tree. Early settlers tell of horses being driven to self-destruction as a result of coming into contact with the plant.

CONVERSATIONAL STYLE

The Stinging Tree

Watch out—this bush bites!

This innocent looking bush may look like a raspberry bush,
with heart-shaped leaves and fleshy red berries.

Don't be fooled!

The innocent looks hide a dangerous weapon—fine,
glass-like hairs which contain a nasty poison.

If you touch a stinging tree, these fine hairs will lodge
in your skin and the poison will cause an intense,
throbbing pain which can last for months!

Even horses have been driven to self-destruction after
touching a stinging tree.

Watch for stinging trees as you walk through the
rainforest. If you see one, stay well clear!!

Figure 4.2: Changing to a conversational style in text

everyday life of visitors. When designing a new exhibition on scientific instruments for the Manchester Museum of Science and Industry, the project team decided to organize the display around topics such as weather forecasting, consumer protection, and health. More than 90 percent of the comments made about the exhibition in a visitor book were very positive.

4. **Giving visitors opportunities to ask questions and make choices.** The previous sections have already described many ways to give visitors opportunities to control information and choose options which interest them the most.

IDEAS FOR CONNECTING TO VISITORS

The main points are:
1. Make personal connections to your visitors:
   - engage them in conversations,
   - use analogies and metaphors from their everyday lives,
   - tell stories with characters they can relate to, and
   - choose topics within everyday experience.
2. Allow visitors some control:
   - give them choices,
   - ask them what interests them, and
   - encourage them to participate.
3. Try to make activities multisensory and dynamic.
4. Visitor attention will be attracted to extreme stimuli, movement and contrast, opportunities for participation, novelty and surprise, and topics of personal relevance.

Providing Variety

Repetition can lead to mindlessness in almost any profession . . . A familiar structure or rhythm helps lead to mental laziness, acting as a signal that there is no need to pay attention. The rhythm of the familiar lulls us into mindlessness:

Q.   *What do we call the tree that grows from acorns?*
A.   *Oak.*
Q.   *What do we call a funny story?*
A.   *Joke.*
Q.   *What do we call the sound made by a frog?*
A.   *Croak.*
Q.   *What do we call the white of an egg?*
A.   *Yolk (sic!).*

(Langer, 1989, pp. 21-22)

Alternatively,
Another subject was given the task of writing ababab ... until he had had enough. He went on until he was mentally and physically exhausted. His hand felt numb, as though it couldn't move to make even one more mark. At that moment the investigator asked him to sign his name and address for a different purpose. He did so quite easily. He was not feigning exhaustion. Rather, the change of context brought renewed energy.

(Langer, 1989, p. 136)

PROVIDING VARIETY in the experiences offered to visitors may seem an obvious point. It is a widely accepted argument that the desire for variety, for a change from routines, is a common motivation for tourism and recreation. Yet repetition is a common feature of many tourist and recreation settings. Around the coast of Australia there are many mangrove areas, and it seems virtually all of them offer a boardwalk with interpretive signs. A visitor from North America, when asked if she would like to go on a mangrove boardwalk, replied, "I've already seen enough mangrove boardwalks to last a lifetime, and they all told me how the

CHAPTER 5: OVERVIEW

AIMS	MAJOR THEMES	SECTIONS WILL PROVIDE
1. To demonstrate the importance of variety in visitor experiences.	**Variety is a critical method for encouraging mindfulness.**	Evidence that variety is desirable.
2. To review ways of including greater variety in visitor experiences.	**Communication with visitors can be varied along many different dimensions.**	A set of features of communication activities that can be changed to provide variety. Examples of providing variety.

roots breathe and how important they are for fish. But basically I'm sick of them and I'm not interested anymore." I am sure we have all heard about, or had, similar experiences where there is simply too much of the same thing. So how can interpreters and communicators make sure they provide variety? That is the question to be addressed in this chapter.

VARIETY IS THE SPICE OF LIFE

The positive benefits of a change in pace or style in an interpretive setting or activity is clear in the comments of visitors themselves. In the Smithsonian Institution in Washington, D.C., an evaluation study found positive responses for Discovery Corners which offered both contact with a guide and the opportunity for interaction with objects. When asked why the experience was so positively rated, it was common in visitors' answers to find references to these being a different experience or change of pace to the other activities and exhibits available. In the words of the visitors:

> *It breaks the monotony of pace—which is good.*
> *I never saw a presentation anything like this in a museum before.*
> *It wouldn't be good to have these all over the place but here and there it gives you something different to do.*
> *(Wolf, Munley, and Tymitz, 1979, pp. 33-34)*

Research conducted in other settings also demonstrates the problems that can result from repetitive experiences. A study of visitors on one-week holidays at tropical island resorts, for example, found a clear link between the patterns or types of activity visitors were offered and their enjoyment (Pearce, 1981). In this particular case, significant increases in negative moods were consistently reported by visitors on the second and third days of their stays. An examination of their activity patterns showed that for the first three days, most of the activities engaged in were structured, social, often physically active, entertainment experiences offered by the resorts. When visitors began to change their activities to include a variety of experiences (such as solitary walks, reading, sunbathing, and interpretive talks), there was a corresponding increase in positive moods.

In both these studies, the evidence clearly supports the author's and Langer's argument that variety is a critical factor in encouraging mindfulness and enjoyment or satisfaction. But what features of communication and interpretation activities can be varied?

DIMENSIONS OF CHANGE

The tropical resort study suggested five features of tourist activities that could be varied:

1. How structured they were, in terms of set times and locations,
2. How social they were, in terms of whether or not the activity had to be done with a group,
3. The focus of the activity as entertainment rather than education,
4. The level of physical activity required, and
5. The level of individual control over the pace and nature of the experience.

The author of this study went on to examine different dimensions of tourist

---

Enjoyable / not enjoyable
Active / passive
Observing / participating
Indoors / outdoors
Individual / group
Crowded / isolated
Water based / land based
Educational / not educational
Relaxing / exciting
Structured / unstructured
No physical effort / physical effort required
Expensive / cheap
Planned / unplanned
Interesting / boring
Manmade setting / natural environment
Daytime / night time
Safe / dangerous
Needs equipment / doesn't need equipment

Notes:
1. Bold features are those directly under manager/operator influence.
2. Italicized features may be able to be influenced.
3. Features are presented in order of importance to those surveyed.

Table 5.1: Features or dimensions of tourist activities

activities by asking people to think about and compare sets of activities. The results, which are listed in Table 5.1, were lists of features of tourist activities that could be varied. Those highlighted in bold in the table are features that can be influenced by managers (Pearce and Moscardo, 1989). The following list is an adaptation of these features or dimensions for communication or interpretive activities.

Activities such as guided tours and visits to zoos, museums, aquaria, visitor centers, and parks can vary in terms of:

1. The senses required, such as vision, touch, and smell.
2. The social nature of the experience. Can it be done alone or must it be with a group?
3. The level of physical activity or effort required.
4. The level of mental activity or challenge required.
5. The degree of emphasis placed on educational content. Is it obvious the visitor should be learning something, or is the focus of the activity on having fun or simply experiencing a place?
6. Features of the physical setting. Is it indoors or outdoors, big or small?
7. The media used. Is it a guided tour, a video, a sign, or a computer display?
8. The level of structure in terms of the extent to which the visitor controls the pace of the activity.

The following sections will now provide more details and some examples of how these dimensions can be used to provide variety in visitor experiences.

The Senses Required

The value of encouraging visitors to use multiple senses has been discussed at several points already in this book, but in keeping with the goal of making each chapter self-contained, this section will review some examples of communication with visitors which encourage or require the use of several senses.

Brockmeyer et al. (1983) provide an example of adding sensory activities to a guided nature walk. Visitors taking a sensory hike through a park in Columbus, Ohio, were encouraged to touch leaves, to cup their hands behind their ears and focus their hearing, and to taste maple sugar. These visitors gave their tour a significantly higher rating for enjoyment than people who took a walk where observation and listening to the guides were the dominant activities. A critical point to note is that the sensory hike did not simply add senses, it varied the use of senses. Adding sound to museum exhibits and zoo displays has also been found to be a positive feature (see Ogden et al., 1993).

The Social Nature of the Experience

One of the more interesting findings in the Brockmeyer et al. (1983) study of sensory and non-sensory walks was that there was less social interaction on the sensory walk. Others have noted that a decrease in social interaction can be associated with interactive exhibits (Brockmeyer et al., 1983; Gillies and Wilson, 1982).

Several authors have expressed concern over this, noting that many visitors are seeking a social experience. It is interesting to note that more recent studies have failed to find any decline in social interaction associated with participatory exhibits (Hilke et al., 1988; Hilke, 1989; Blud, 1990).

Still, it could be argued that few interpretive activities actively encourage social interaction. Even guided tours (especially short ones), which by default include a group, rarely explicitly require visitors to do anything together. One exception is the salt mine tours in the mountains near Salzburg in Austria. Visitors are required to get a partner, and at various points in the tour the pair must engage in activities together, such as sliding down from level to level in complete darkness. At other times the partner is not required. Another example is a cruise available through the wetlands and mangroves of North Queensland, Australia. At various points in the cruise, the guide asks different groups of people to do certain activities, such as preparing tea or baiting crab pots. Sometimes the groups are made up of visitors already traveling together and sometimes the guide constructs the groups himself. The tour also includes two opportunities for the visitors to be by themselves. At one point, they are encouraged to spend some time alone simply soaking up the atmosphere.

Group size on this tour is usually less than 12, while salt mine tour groups are rarely less than 30. Group size is another feature that can be varied.

Level of Physical Activity Required

At one end of this dimension are activities such as sitting in theaters watching audiovisual presentations, sitting while reading reference material (an increasingly popular option in visitor centers), or sitting in a bus or boat and watching scenery or wildlife. At the other end are adventure activities such as rafting, diving, and climbing which require extensive and intensive physical exertion. In between, there are many options. Many visitor centers and museums now include participatory exhibits which require varying levels of physical activity from participants. The British Museum of Natural History's presentation on elephants and animal movement, for example, has displays which ask visitors to press down columns to feel the pressure supported by different anatomical structures.

Many places and many tours, however, seem to settle quickly into a steady pattern of activity, with visitors walking at a slow to moderate pace, punctuated with stops where visitors stand or sit to listen, read, or watch. I attended a conference recently where the organizers punctuated a particularly long session of papers with a very brief and gentle aerobics session led by an entertaining physical trainer. Many first reactions were that this seemed a little silly, but the overwhelming final reaction was that it was a very enjoyable and energizing experience.

Level of Mental Activity or Challenge Required

Asking visitors questions requires a different level of mental activity than asking them to listen to someone talking. Using a computer quiz program can be more challenging than reading a small sign. Questions can also vary in level of difficulty. For some questions, the answer might be found further in the text, while for others there may be no single answer, and it may not be able to be answered from the information immediately available. The amount of information a guide includes in a tour can vary from a few simple messages to very detailed and complex explanations. Each of these is an example of varying the level of mental activity required.

The Degree of Emphasis Placed on Educational Content

This dimension or feature is not unrelated to the previous one, and to some readers it may seem contradictory. Virtually all of the examples of communication or interpretive activities that have been used thus far have had the clear goal of imparting information to visitors. But not every aspect of a guided tour, a tourist attraction, or an interpretive center need have a specific educational content. Sometimes an activity or part of an activity can be simply fun or can be concerned with the direct experience of a place. Participants in the Salzburg salt mining tour regularly moved from level to level in the mine by whizzing down dark slides, holding onto their partner. This activity was pure fun. Night animal spotlighting tours in the tropical rainforests of North Queensland often include a break where visitors can sit quietly in the dark listening to and feeling the forest at night. It has been suggested that many tourist attractions provide fun at the expense of education. But it could be just as easily argued that many park rangers and museum guides emphasize education at the expense of fun.

Features of the Physical Setting

Where possible, features of the physical setting can be changed to create different atmospheres and different experiences. The Cradle Mountain National Park Visitor Center combines indoor and outdoor settings to create varied experiences. Visitors to this center in Tasmania, Australia, can access a short, temperate, rainforest walk from within the center. The path returns them to the center where they can continue through the displays. The Royal Tyrrell Museum of Paleontology in Alberta, Canada, provides considerable variety in its physical settings. This popular museum provides small and large exhibition spaces, outdoor boardwalks, and a large, indoor cycad and fern garden. Some spaces are like traditional museum galleries with cases containing objects and signs, and text and illustrations on the walls. Other spaces contain large dioramas which contain replicas of excavations and reconstructed dinosaurs. Knowing the layout of one section gives you no idea about the layout of any other section. In each new section you have to think again about what you are going to do.

Readers accustomed to communicating with visitors in natural environments may find it difficult to contemplate ways to alter the physical setting. But sometimes such opportunities will be available. The design of new walks and trails, for example, offers an opportunity to expose visitors to different types of environment. Anecdotal evidence suggests that visitors prefer walks that take them through different kinds of places.

Interpreters can also capitalize on naturally occurring changes in the physical setting, such as day versus night, seasonal differences, and low versus high tide. The same place can provide different experiences at different times of the day and of the year. Even quite subtle variations have the potential to provide varied visitor experiences.

The Media Used

Built attractions and settings such as museums, historic sites, and visitor centers increasingly use a variety of media for communicating with their visitors. Slides, audiovisuals, text, illustrations, computers, books, and talks are commonly available in these places. Guides, however, tend not to use anything more than themselves and objects taken from the setting to present information to visitors. I have experienced, however, tours where the guide used recorded sounds to enliven a presentation of a historical site. I have also seen guides distribute books and reference materials to visitors at rest and lunch stops, encouraging them to pursue personal interests and ask questions.

The Level of Structure

By structure, we mean the extent to which the visitor, rather than the communicator, has control over the pace, content, and direction of the activity. Many guided tours, for example, are very structured, starting at set places and times and covering set routes. In many cases there are good and necessary reasons for having structure. But in some cases, the structure results more from habit than from need. It is worth contemplating points where visitors can be given some control over the pace and direction of the activities.

An Important Note

It is important to remember that the critical element in all these examples is variety. It is not the case that one end of any of these dimensions is better or preferable to the other. Thus passive, structured experiences are not to be considered as either better or worse than active, unstructured ones. Rather, the critical point is that mindfulness is most likely to be encouraged when some variety exists on any of these dimensions.

PUTTING IT ALL TOGETHER: SOME EXAMPLES

The following three case studies provide examples of tourist and recreation places that offer interpretive and environmental activities which are varied on numerous dimensions:

Head Smashed in Buffalo Jump

This World Heritage site in Alberta, Canada, offers visitors a major interpretive center, a walk to a viewing area near the top of the cliff, (which was the jump site), and walks around the base of the cliff. Volunteers are available to tell stories and answer visitors' questions at the clifftop viewing area. Inside the center are a variety of displays, including traditional standing displays with text and illustrations, audiovisuals, interactive computer displays, and objects in cases. In one section, text is projected down onto a series of stones from the ceiling. It is a common media or presentation technique turned literally on its side to create quite a different experience. Members of First Nation groups connected to the site also tell stories at various times in the center. From time to time, visitors can also converse with archeologists excavating sections of the site.

In summary, the site provides outdoor and indoor experiences, somewhat structured (listening to the volunteers and storytellers) experiences and unstructured opportunities to walk around the site, a variety of media, and different levels of both physical and mental activity.

Skyrail Cableway

This rainforest cableway in the tropical rainforests of Far North Eastern Australia (see Chapters One and Four for other discussions of this site) takes visitors from the coastal plain over rainforest-covered mountains to a village at the top of a major river gorge. The cableway runs for seven and a half kilometers and visitors are able to leave the cable cars or gondolas at two stations in the rainforest. At one station, visitors can walk through the rainforest on a raised boardwalk which provides several information or interpretive signs. Uniformed guides are also available to take people on tours of the rainforest boardwalk. Displays and touch tables on rainforest seeds and fruits are also offered for visitors at this station. The second station provides a short walk and lookouts over a waterfall and gorge. A Rainforest Interpretive Center can also be found at this second station. This center has touch tables, audiovisuals, interactive computer exhibits, and displays. Again, staff are available at the lookouts to answer questions.

In this example, there is variety in the media used, indoor and outdoor experiences, structured and unstructured activities, and variety in terms of mental activity required. Currently, the interpretive staff are developing a seasonal diary which can be used to help visitors notice seasonal variations in the rainforest.

St. Kilda Mangrove Boardwalk, South Australia

This boardwalk is located on the southern coast of Australia just to the west of Adelaide. The boardwalk provides visitors with experiences which vary along several dimensions. Firstly, the boardwalk incorporates several bird hides where visitors are encouraged to sit quietly and watch the bird life. Visitors are assisted by identification guides inside the hides. Secondly, for most of the walk, the boardwalk is just above the high-tide water level, but in several places it rises to the tops of the trees to allow for a different perspective. At one point, visitors have the option of climbing up a ladder to a platform above the tree tops and looking out over the mangroves to the open ocean. The option of the platform provides both a more physically active experience and a different perspective on the setting. Visitors on the walk can take with them a brochure which asks questions and suggests activities. At one point, for example, the brochure requests the reader to lie on the boardwalk and listen for the popping noises made when oxygen bubbles are released by the algae in the water.

OTHER BENEFITS OF PROVIDING VARIETY

In addition to encouraging mindfulness in visitors, variety in the experiences offered to visitors has several other benefits for tourism and recreation settings. Firstly, variety can often provide visitors with some choice over what they experience, thus introducing some options for visitors to take some control over the activities. Secondly, providing variety in the experiences offered may allow an attraction or a site to match the expectations of a wider variety of audiences or visitors. An example from the rainforest areas of North Queensland can help illustrate this point. Various surveys of visitors to this region have identified two main types of rainforest visitors: a high activity group who would like to participate in physically challenging activities and to get close to wildlife and nature; and a general sightseeing group seeking more quiet, relaxing, and passive experiences. The second group was found to be highly satisfied with the rainforest experiences available in the region. The first group, however, had significantly lower satisfaction scores. An examination of their answers to open-ended questions suggested that one of the major causes of this lower satisfaction was a perception that all available rainforest sites provided the same experience. An analysis of the most popular sites confirms this perception. Many of them offer a picnic area, scenic viewing, and short walks, and most have a similar configuration of carparks, walks, and facilities (see Moscardo, 1996c, for further details).

Thirdly, variety can be an important component for attracting repeat visitors. If visitors believe that the experience offered at a place is repetitive and unlikely to change, then they will be less interested in visiting that place again. The Skyrail attraction provides a good example of the potential power of variety for encouraging repeat visitation. A survey of Skyrail visitors found that 62 percent of international visitors would repeat the experience if they returned to the region, 75 percent of domestic visitors would repeat the experience, and 42 percent of local residents intended to repeat the experience within 12 months.

REPEATING THE MAIN POINTS

Variety is a key element in encouraging mindfulness and enhancing the quality of visitor experiences.

Communication or interpretation activities can be varied along a number of dimensions, including:
  - the senses required,
  - the social nature of the experience,
  - the level of physical activity required,
  - the level of mental activity required,

- the media used, and
- the features of the physical setting.

Variety can also give visitors a sense of control and a reason to return, and can help managers meet the needs of a varied audience.

6

Telling a Good Story That Makes Sense

If the balloons popped the sound wouldn't be able to carry since everything would be too far away from the correct floor. A closed window would also prevent the sound from carrying, since most buildings tend to be well insulated. Since the whole operation depends on a steady flow of electricity, a break in the middle of the wire would also cause problems. Of course, the fellow could shout, but the human voice is not loud enough to carry that far. An additional problem is that a string could break on the instrument. Then there could be no accompaniment to the message. It is clear that the best situation would involve less distance. Then there would be fewer potential problems. With face to face contact, the least number of things could go wrong.

(Bransford and Johnson, 1973, pp. 392-393)

DOES THIS PASSAGE make any sense to you? Could you suggest what the topic is? Probably not. But perhaps it might if you look ahead to Figure 6.3 at the end of this chapter and then read the passage again.

Now it makes sense. This is an old teaching trick in psychology. The point is that the passage makes sense when the full context is given. No matter how mindful you are, without the context it is nonsense. Psychologists would refer to this context as a schema. The drawing activates our schema for a serenade, and we can then make sense of the passage. It is schemata (the plural for schema) that we use all the time to function in our world. We all have a schema for dogs, for furniture, and for watching television. In these schemata, we have knowledge about dogs or furniture, we have memories of past experiences with them, and we often have some emotional responses to them. We use these schemata to guide our behavior whenever we encounter dogs or furniture. We build schema through experiences. When my son was first learning to speak he had a broad schema that could be labeled "animals in people's yards." He used the word "dog" to include dogs, horses, cats, geese, bicycles, and cattle. They were all dogs. He had a simple schema for non-human things in yards. The more experience we have, the more detailed our schemata become.

CHAPTER 6: OVERVIEW

AIMS	MAJOR THEMES	SECTIONS WILL PROVIDE
1. To demonstrate ideas for organizing information for visitors. 2. To consider ways of finding a common ground for communicating with visitors.	**Making visitors mindful is a good start to ensuring effective communication, but all your efforts will be wasted if you confuse people.** **There are two main ways you can confuse visitors.** **1. Through poor organization of information.** **2. Through not knowing what visitors know.**	Some insights into visitor preferences for different ways of organizing information. Examples of ways information can be structured, including stories and themes. Some research into the problems of finding common ground with visitors.

Interpretation and communication are often trying to build or renovate visitors' schemata. You are trying to give your visitors a schema or trying to change the one they already have. You're trying to give them information that will make sense and that they can use to guide them in their subsequent dealings with some place or topic. Making sense is what this chapter is about. The basic argument is that you can make people mindful, but you will not change what they know or think if your information or message is confusing or poorly organized. Thinking again of ourselves as travelers or explorers, we know that if we want the people in the places we visit to understand us, we have to do more than simply speak louder.

WHAT DO VISITORS LIKE?

A small number of studies have been conducted into visitor preferences for topics and ways of organizing information. Washburne and Wagar (1972), in what could be described as one of the classics in visitor research, interviewed visitors in four centers in National Parks and Forests in the Pacific Northwest of the United States. These visitors were asked to nominate the exhibit that they found to be the most interesting. The researchers then looked at various characteristics of these exhibits. The results indicated that visitors preferred information presented as cause-and-effect relationships or as a story, and they preferred information that was related to their immediate surroundings. The visitors in this study did not like information presented as isolated facts or as identification. Prince (1982) repeated this study with visitors to two centers in the North York Moore National Park in the United Kingdom. His results were the same.

Walker (1988) reports on research into visitor perspectives on exhibits designed for the Royal Ontario Museum. The results of this research found that visitors preferred objects to be presented with information about them organized as a story, and that they liked the objects to be presented in an appropriate context. A piece of furniture, for example, should be presented as part of a room.

In summary it seems that visitors prefer:
- to be told stories,
- to have the relationships between pieces of information made clear, and
- to be able to make connections between information and a larger context.

Lessons from Psychology

The visitor preferences reported in the previous section are consistent with research and theory in areas of psychology concerned with understanding how people think and learn. We have previously used the word schema. Schemata are the mental frameworks we use to organize past experience and information. Learning new information can be seen as the building and renovating of these schemata. Psychologists use the term *assimilation* to describe one of the processes involved in renovating existing schemata. We assimilate new information by connecting it to what we already know (Myers, 1986). This may partly explain visitor preferences for the use of familiar objects or connections to everyday experience in communication and interpretation. Not only are these objects and experiences more relevant, they are also easier to understand. Visitor preferences for having information connected to a larger context is also consistent with this process of assimilation.

Another way we can change schemata is through a process referred to as accommodation. Assimilation fits new information into the existing frameworks. Accommodation involves changing the framework to fit the new information. In an earlier section, I talked about my son and his early **schema** for "dogs." Clearly, his first schema could be described as "non-human moving objects that could be found around houses." He began with his experiences in his own yard where he could find two dogs. His parents obligingly gave him the label *dog* for these non-human moving objects. As he gathered more experiences from visits to neighbors and walks with his parents, he encountered new examples of these non-human moving objects, such as horses, cats, and bicycles. He was able to **assimilate** these new examples. They all shared the key features of being moving and non-human, and so he used the label "dogs" for them all.

Increasing experience of dogs, bicycles, and horses, however, began to challenge this simple schema. Bicycles and horses, for example, could be found outside yards and they could carry people. He also found that dogs would eat his leftover peanut butter sandwiches, but no matter how hard he tried, the bicycle was not interested in them. It became clear that his single, simple schema did not fit. These creatures had less in common than he had thought, so he had to **accommodate** this information by developing new schema for each.

One way to **accommodate** is to borrow the structure of an existing schema. Stories are a good example of a common and easily borrowed structure, and this may be one reason for their popularity. Another reason is that it is difficult to tell a story without using concrete or specific examples, and there is increasing evidence from psychology research that we often have difficulties with abstract concepts, especially in unfamiliar areas.

The psychologist responsible for the concepts of assimilation and accommodation was Jean Piaget. Piaget was also responsible for a widely accepted theory of cognitive development (Myers, 1986). In this theory, Piaget suggested four basic stages that all humans go through as they grow from infants to adults. Table 6.1 summarizes these stages. Of particular interest to the present discussion are the last two stages, called *Concrete* and *Formal Operational*. In both stages, people are able to think logically. The main difference between the two is that in the first, our thinking is limited to concrete, specific objects, events, or places, while in the second, we can think about abstract concepts. An example can help explain this difference.

Recently, a young teenage relative came to visit for a holiday. Shortly after she arrived, I found myself to be an object of intense interest to her. I would often find her staring at me intensely. So I asked her what was wrong. Her reply was surprising. She was looking for evidence that I was being physically abused. When I asked her why she should expect that this was the case, she replied, "I was watching TV and this man said that domestic violence occurs in one out of three households and you live in the sixth house from the end of the street." She had translated an abstract concept into a concrete reality!

Although Piaget argued that all adults reach this Formal Operational stage, more recent evidence suggests that many of us never do. Further, it seems that even if we have the capacity to think and reason with abstract concepts, we rarely do. In particular, we are very likely to be concrete thinkers in new and unfamiliar settings (Myers, 1986). The implication for communicators is that visitors will find it easier to follow concrete examples.

INFORMATION DESIGN TO HELP VISITORS UNDERSTAND

Approximate Age	Stage
Birth - 2 years	Sensorimotor: Infant experiences the world through senses.
2 - 6 years	Preoperational: Children can talk about things, but do not think logically.
7 - 12 years	Concrete Operational: Children can think logically about concrete events.
13 onwards	Formal Operational: People are able to reason abstractly.

(From Myers, 1986, p. 70)

Table 6.1: A summary of Piaget's stages of cognitive development

Orientation or Advance Organizers

There are several factors to consider in the organization of content. Firstly there is a need to provide visitors with some mental orientation or overview. Many studies have demonstrated the benefits of providing visitors with an introduction which gives an overview of the interpretive activity and explains the organization of the content. In an earlier section, it was argued that the use of questions on signs or in talks was an effective method for encouraging mindfulness. Questions can also help visitors learn by highlighting the main or important points to be learned.

Two studies provide direct evidence that questions can act as cognitive orientation devices and thus enhance learning. In a study conducted at the Florida State Museum (Lehman and Lehman, 1984), undergraduate students were given instructions to observe an exhibit carefully, read the information available in the exhibit, and answer some questions that were given to them. Or they could observe the exhibit, read the information, generate their own questions, and answer these. While both groups who answered questions did better on a test on the exhibit content than a control group who did not answer questions, the group answering the questions given to them before the exhibit was experienced did best of all three groups. In a similar study also conducted with students visiting the Florida State Museum, Koran et al. (1983b) asked students to study some questions either before or after entering a display area. The results revealed that both these groups of students had significantly higher mean scores than a group having no questions, and that the group who studied the questions before entering the display area had the highest mean score. Thus, it seems that questions can enhance learning, particularly if they are presented before an exhibit is experienced.

The use of questions is one way of providing cognitive orientation to interpretation. Another is the use of previsit instructions. Gennaro (1981) and Gennaro et al. (1984), for example, provided evidence from several studies supporting the value of previsit instructions on how to visit a museum for enhancing learning from a museum.

This is consistent with research in education into the use of what are called *advance organizers*. The available evidence clearly shows that advance organizers enhance learning (Healy, 1989; Spiegel and Barufaldi, 1994). So what are advance organizers? Advance organizers tell the visitor how information is structured or organized. According to Wurman, "knowing how to look for information gives you the freedom to find it" (1989, p. 52). Advance organizers are like maps: they provide an overview and introduction to the material that is to be presented. They usually provide a summary of the main points to be presented and often include instructions on how to deal with the information available.

The chapter previews given at the beginning of each chapter in this book are examples of advance organizers. An introductory speech by a guide that gives visitors an outline of the tour and what is going to happen is another example of an advance organizer. A brochure given to visitors before they start a tour can be an advance organizer if it includes an overview or outline of the tour and/or gives instructions on how to approach the tour. Figure 6.1 gives some examples of ad-

A. An introductory sign in a state forest, Australia

LACEY CREEK State Forest Park

Lacey Creek is one of two areas developed for visitors to Tam O'Shanter State Forest. The park contains lush coastal lowland rainforest. A walking track takes you through this environment and highlights points of interest. One of Queensland's highest concentrations of the graceful rainforest bird, the southern cassowary, is found in the park. You may be fortunate and see one during your visit.

Map of Area

Things to see and do
Walking
A 1.1 km rainforest circuit track commences at the car park. Trailside information is provided. Allow 40 minutes for the walk.

Nature Study
A rich array of birds is found in the rainforest, including the southern cassowary.

PLEASE REMEMBER

The cassowary is a wild animal. Please do not feed cassowaries.

Stay on marked tracks.

B. A simple introduction to a self-guided trail

Tropical rainforest
Tropical rainforest is one of nature's most complex biological systems. This self-guided walk introduces some of the rainforest's plants and animals and the fascinating ways they interact.

Illustration of
Rainforest Plants

C. An example of a possible introduction to a guided walk

This walk is going to show you how tropical rainforests respond to clearing. The walk is about 3 kilometers, and it will take us about two hours.

Some of the land along this walk was completely cleared about 50 years ago for farming. Other sections were selectively logged. Some of the land has been left untouched for about 30 years. This means that along the walk we will be able to see different stages of rainforest regeneration.

Figure 6.1: Examples of advance organizers

vance organizers for self-guiding trails in North Queensland's rainforests. Another example is the introductory exhibit (an advance organizer) in a visitor center in the Rocky Mountains National Park in the United States. In this center (see Chapter 1 for further details), information is organized first into the activities available in the park. Each activity, such as bird-watching, walking, and photography, has its own exhibit. Each exhibit has information organized into several layers. These layers provide information on opportunities available in the park for people spending a short time, a day, or several days in the area. Each layer is color coded. An introductory exhibit explains this system to visitors. Visitor studies found "a two-to-one preference for the map/organizer versus the information counter" for information and assistance (Mack and Thompson, 1991, p. 116).

Advance organizers can:
- tell us what to look for,
- provide us with a general schema to fit new information into,
- identify the main points, and
- help us make connections between pieces of information.

Themes

Themes provide a single focus or core item to which all other information is linked. Animals in zoos can be housed in areas according to habitat. The habitat becomes the theme, and the various individual animal displays can be linked to that place. Historical interpretation is often presented as an historical progression, where the timeline becomes the theme or thread that links various parts of the interpretation. Themes are a commonly used device in tourist and recreation settings. The key to their success lies in choosing themes that are appealing to visitors and which make clear connections to the information being presented.

Stories

Stories are a particularly effective way to present information. But what exactly is a story? According to the *Oxford English Dictionary* it is many things, including a "course of events," a "descriptive piece of news," the "main facts," or "factors or experiences that deserve narration" (1982, p. 1050). An examination of descriptions of stories and guidance for writing and telling stories, available on the World Wide Web (WWW), gives some more interesting and meaningful perspectives. According to a guide found on the WWW for presenting stories, a story must have an introduction, a scene, a protagonist, a climax, and an ending (Anonymous, 1996). Following this pattern may seem easy if the content involves humans, but it is not so obvious how this fits if the interpretation is about a topic such as geology. Yet Frack (1996) provides a guide for schoolchildren which makes several suggestions for writing stories about rocks. The most basic of these suggestions is to make the rock the protagonist and to tell the story as an autobiography beginning, say, with magma and ending with where the rock is now. This may seem childish, but it is not necessary to make the rock animated or to identify the interpretation as a story in order for the essential elements to remain. In the words of another WWW

A. Example of List of Facts Approach	B. Example of a Story Approach
The Curtain Fig Tree (Ficus virens) **Stages in the development of the Curtain Fig Tree** 1. A seed is deposited in the host tree's crown in bird droppings. The seed germinates and its first root begins to descend to the soil. 2. Enriched by the soil, the fig develops aerial roots which encircle and eventually strangle the host tree. 3. This stage is unique in the development of the Curtain Fig Tree. The host tree fell into a neighboring tree. Vertical fig roots descended from its leaning trunk to form the curtain-like appearance. 4. Eventually the host tree rots away, leaving the free-standing fig tree. **Fig Tree Facts** Age: About 500 years Height: Nearly 50 meters Trunk Circumference: About 39 meters Fruits: Fleshy black or purple fruits are produced during wet season. Leaves: Most leaves fall for up to one month late in the dry season.	**Cathedral Facts** A strangler fig such as the Cathedral Fig starts life high in the forest canopy, where a seed is dropped by a bird or bat into the fork of a tree. The seed germinates and the fig may live on high as an epiphyte for many years. When conditions are favorable, the fig sends fine, cable-like roots down the host's trunk to the ground. Roots act as a feeding tube, and the plant grows rapidly. Roots fuse to encircle the host tree. By restricting the sap flow to canopy leaves, the strangler fig may finally kill its host. Strangler figs are a common feature of upland tropical rainforests. **How Big?** At 50 meters, the Cathedral Fig stands head and shoulders above the other rainforest trees. This is the same height as a 12-story building. The crown of the Cathedral Fig extends over 0.2 hectare. This is the same size as two Olympic swimming pools. Roots extend over one hectare. It is 43 meters around the Fig. If 24 people linked hands around the tree they would just meet together. The Cathedral Fig carries a heavy load of leaves equivalent to the weight of a small elephant. **By Day** As the sun rises, the dawn chorus heralds the start of a new day. The Cathedral Fig comes alive. In season, fruit-eating pigeons and parrots feed noisily in the canopy above. Reptiles emerge from the security of their night-time den to hunt for food. Nocturnal animals rely on the tree for a safe day-time roost. Owls, bandicoots, and bettong all seek refuge in the fig's protective shelter. As the day progresses, activity quiets as animals try to escape the heat. At dusk, activity is again at fever pitch as the day shift retires and nocturnal animals awaken. **By Night** The face of the fig changes at night. There is much activity, but most occurs in silence. Night-time spotlighting can be rewarding. Opossums and tree kangaroos relish fig leaves. At least five varieties of opossums can be found around the fig. Aerial roots used as roosts during the day become perches for owls for night-time hunting activities. In season, fig fruit is eagerly sought by flying foxes and opossums.

Figure 6.2: Two approaches to a similar topic

author, a story describes a process or tells us about what happens (Flemming, 1996). Figure 6.2 provides an example of two different approaches to presenting a similar attraction. The one on the right tells a story.

FINDING COMMON GROUND

In addition to organizing information, effective communicators need to find a common ground with their audience. In order to change people's existing knowledge, we need to know what they already know. In Chapter 2, we noted that there were three possible situations that can occur when communicators and audiences come together:

1. The information presented is either so unfamiliar or abstract that the audience cannot make sense of it. They simply cannot fit it anywhere in

A. Text from an Art Exhibition

Some of the most radical and influential movements of 20th-century art can be identified with the Russian avant-garde—the experimental artists who invented and developed ideas such as Rayonnism (Mikhail Larionov and Natalia Gontcharova), Suprematism (Kasimir Malevich, Ivan Kliunkov, Kliun, Ivan Puni) and Constructivism (Vladimir Tatlin, Lazar (El) Lissitzky, Alexander Rodchenko, Liubov Popova, Alexandra Exter, Naum Gabo).	Perhaps the most astonishing characteristic of the Russian avant-garde is the swiftness with which its representatives absorbed and developed styles such as French Cubism and Italian Futurism, combining them with indigenous cultural traditions and arriving at unique pictorial conclusions. For example, the dramatic shift from figurative to non-figurative art occurred almost overnight—with Tatlin's creation of his first abstract relief early in 1914 and with the public showing of Malevichy's famous Black Square at the exhibition "0.10" in Petrograd in 1915.

(Chambers, 1984, p. 49)

B. Text from a Sign on a Self-Guided Trail

The rocks here in Mobo Creek are basalt, suggesting a previous flow from a volcanic crater.
The mystery is that the basalt rocks appear to be flowing into, rather than out of the crater. Also, the steep walls of the crater consist of non-volcanic rocks rather than the expected basalt.
One explanation is that the crater represents the remnant of an underground basalt formation. Over time, the waters of Mobo Creek have eroded the non-volcanic rock above this formation, exposing the basalt rock. Hence the basalt rock now forms the creek base with the non-volcanic rock walls above. The flow of basalt may appear inwards as only part of the formation is exposed.

(Selected from a sign on Mobo Creek Crater Walk, Danbulla State Forest, Australia)

**Table 6.2: Examples of communication that assume
expert knowledge exists in the audience**

their existing knowledge frameworks. This is a common problem in art museums, where many communicators believe that the art will speak for itself (Dobbs, 1990). Table 6.2 gives an example of text used in an art exhibition. Chambers (1984) argues that text is unreadable. Comprehension of this label would require a very detailed knowledge of, and background in, art history. Table 6.2 also contains an example of some natural history text from a self-guided walking trail which arguably would be very difficult to follow for someone who did not have a geological background.

2. The second possibility is that visitors have quite detailed knowledge frameworks or schemata which conflict with or contradict the information presented by the communicator. In this case, the audience can and will adapt the information to suit their existing systems. The unintended outcome of such an encounter may be that the communicator reinforces pre-existing and inaccurate schemata.

These pre-existing schemata have been called misconceptions or naive theories, and there is growing evidence that many people, including college graduates, have misconceptions or inaccurate, naive theories of many biological and physical concepts. Munson (1994), for example, provides a review of common misconceptions of such things as ecosystems, food chains, and photosynthesis. Minda Borun and her colleagues have conducted many studies into visitor responses to communication about physics topics such as gravity (Borun et al., 1993; Borun, 1991; Borun and Adams, 1991). Borun concludes:

One of the unanticipated problems we've encountered in studying and working with naive notions is the reluctance of experts to accept the existence and prevalence of these notions. It has been difficult to explain that people really believe that if the earth stopped spinning, gravity would cease and we would fall off into space! Our experts seem to persist in thinking that what's needed is an exhibit that demonstrates what gravity is. Our research, on the other hand, shows that about half of our visitors are not able to understand what gravity is until they see what gravity is not. (1991, p. 11)

Griggs provides another interesting example of the importance of this factor in his description of a study conducted by the British Museum of Natural History into visitor knowledge, as part of the development of a dinosaur exhibition. The study found that few visitors understood the concepts of natural selection and evolution, which were critical to the planned exhibition. The result was "a decision to redevelop the exhibits from scratch, including writing a new storyline and a new set of objectives" (1982, p. 199).

Figure 6.3: Context or information to make sense of the balloons passage
(Adapted from Bransford & Johnson, 1973)

This problem of conflicting knowledge or theories is also a problem for cross-cultural topics. It may be very difficult to change visitors' pre-existing beliefs about other cultural groups. Statham (1993) provides an example of this problem in his description of British visitors' responses to a traveling exhibition on Japanese culture. He concluded that "responses to the questionnaire also suggested that the exhibition could have done more to counter stereotyped impressions of Japan" (p. 217).

3. The final possibility is that visitors have the relevant pre-existing knowledge and so share a common ground with the communicator. Unfortunately, it is likely that this will rarely be the case.

The lesson to be learned from this research is that communicators need to understand what their visitors already know or believe about a topic.

SUMMING UP

Effective communication needs to be clear and well organized, and effective communicators need to share at least some common ground with their audience. The following features can assist in the creation of effective communication:

- using advance organizers to explain to visitors the structure of the communication, the key points, and how to approach and deal with the information to be presented
- themes and stories are effective ways to structure and organize information

To change visitors' knowledge, we need to have some understanding of the knowledge and beliefs visitors bring with them.

■ 7

Getting to Know Your Visitors

"It was just the painstaking realization that the components of this exhibit that I was so certain had to work, simply didn't work. They not only bored visitors, but frustrated them, which was even worse."
—Alan Friedman, Director of the New York Hall of Science in response to a question asking him how he became convinced that visitor evaluation was a valuable process.

(Hicks, 1986, p. 39)

IN PREVIOUS CHAPTERS, I have made many suggestions for improving the effectiveness or quality of visitor communication efforts. These have included:
- attracting visitor attention through novelty and surprise,
- making personal connections to visitors by providing familiar examples or choosing topics that visitors are interested in, and
- making sure you build upon the knowledge that visitors bring with them.

Each of these principles requires some understanding of visitors and their experiences, motives, and existing knowledge.

If communicators in tourism and recreation settings are going to be effective at providing quality visitor experiences, then they need to get to know their visitors.

WHAT SORTS OF THINGS CAN YOU KNOW ABOUT YOUR VISITORS?

Communicators should be particularly interested in factors which have the potential to influence how visitors respond to a message. The two main categories are the sociodemographic and psychological characteristics that visitors bring with them to tourist and recreation places, and the knowledge that visitors have.

CHAPTER 7: OVERVIEW

AIMS	MAJOR THEMES	SECTIONS WILL PROVIDE
1. To demonstrate the value of collecting information about visitors.	**You need to know who your visitors are, what they know, and what they think of your communication, if you want to have a high-quality product or service.**	Information on visitor characteristics that can influence their responses to communication efforts.
2. To introduce methods for gathering visitor information.	**Visitor evaluation is a critical part of communication.**	An introduction to types and methods of visitor evaluation.

Visitor Characteristics

Communication and interpretation research has generally focussed on characteristics of the communication rather than the audience. The visitor research that has been done has identified three interrelated variables as being the most important. These are familiarity or experience with the setting, motivations or goals, and social interaction.

Familiarity

In the case of familiarity, the work of Falk is predominant. In Balling and Falk (1980) and Falk (1983), it has been demonstrated that visitors who were familiar with a setting, that is, they had visited the setting before, were more likely to learn something than those who were unfamiliar with the setting. These results were consistent with those of Borun (1977) and Prince (1982). The argument is that familiar visitors are better oriented and thus can focus more attention on the communication.

Motives

It may also be the case that experienced visitors have different goals or motives than first-time visitors. A study of visitors to the Denver Art Museum analyzed visitor responses to a series of questions including reasons for visiting, the kind of experience sought, and use of interpretive aids (Edwards et al., 1990). In this study, the authors contrasted High Involvement visitors, who were likely to be repeat visitors and value educational opportunities, with Low Involvement visitors, who were more likely to be novice visitors and to value social interaction. High Involvement visitors sought a wider range of interpretive material such as exhibit catalogues and books on the artwork, and placed more value on information about the artists and the place of a piece of art in art history. The results indicated that the High Involvement visitors had the most detailed pre-existing knowledge.

Social Group

Another variable associated with motives and experience is the social group of the visitor. Hood (1989) found that families were not as interested in education as other visitors. Diamond (1986) concentrated her observations on family groups and found that adults often kept children at exhibits, and engaged in instructive behaviors such as reading and interpreting labels for children. Adults also terminated exhibit interaction and appeared to control the length of the visit. Laetsch et al. (1980) also observed families and found, like Hilke (1989), that adults and children spent more time together than either children with children or adults with other adults. These authors also observed that in family groups, considerable time was given to group management.

While families in museums have prompted much attention (see Hirschi and Screven, 1988; Butler and Sussman, 1989; McManus, 1994; Brown, 1995), only one study has examined in detail the influence of various group compositions on visitor behavior. McManus (1987, 1988) observed 641 visitor groups at the British Museum of Natural History. She found that social units could be placed into four categories which had distinctive patterns of behavior: groups with children, individuals alone, couples, and adult peer groups. Groups with children had the longest visits, longest periods of conversation, were the most likely to use interactive exhibits, and least likely to read text. As with the studies of families discussed previously, McManus suggested that adults modified their behavior to suit children. Couples had the lowest levels of conversation, high levels of reading, long visits, and low use of interactive exhibits. Adult peer groups had the lowest levels of attention to exhibits and few consistent patterns of behavior, while adults alone had the shortest visits, low use of interactive exhibits and displayed the most comprehensive reading of labels. McManus also found that groups with good social cohesion, as measured by the distances maintained between group members, read more and had longer conversations than those with low levels of group cohesion.

Culture

Another factor which is likely to be important is that of the visitor's cultural background. Cultural background has virtually been ignored in visitor studies, yet it is likely to be an increasingly important issue, as more tourism is generated from previously developing countries and as many resident populations become increasingly heterogeneous. Communication with visitors from different cultural backgrounds is likely to face difficulties because of language barriers, differences in patterns of social interaction, differences in values and attitudes, differences in knowledge, and differences in learning styles (see Caro and Ewert, 1995; and Falk, 1995, for reviews of research).

Lee et al. (1995) provide an example of how cultural groups can differ in terms of their knowledge and preferred learning styles. These researchers looked at these variables in four groups of students:

1. monolingual English Caucasian,
2. African-American,

3. bilingual Spanish, and

4. bilingual Haitian Creole.

They found significant differences in the types of knowledge these groups of students had about various science concepts. The greatest differences, however, were in the ways these groups approached learning. The first three groups all used prior knowledge and personal experience to answer science questions. Hispanic students also used strategies of peer collaboration and seeking information from others in their group. African-American students frequently used analogies to try to understand the problems. Haitian Creole students relied heavily on observation and imitation of the presenter. Thus each group approached the situation in a very different way, reflecting different cultural rules about social status and social interaction.

These different cultural rules guiding social interaction can present many problems for communicators. Kim (1996) listed 37 problems that Korean visitors encountered when they visited Australia. Table 7.1 lists some with the potential to create difficulties for communicators. The lack of non-verbal feedback, in particular, can cause difficulties for European communicators who find it hard to determine if the visitors have understood or appreciated their efforts.

The Lee et al. (1995) study also found difficulties in the translation of concepts from English to other languages. This problem was one of several identified in a project which evaluated the use of pictorial symbols for educating different groups of visitors about appropriate behaviors in reef environments (Moscardo et al., 1997). One of the problems facing the managers of Australia's Great Barrier Reef is that there has been a substantial increase in recent years in the number of non-English speaking visitors. One proposed solution to the problem of presenting information in multiple languages was the development of pictorial symbols or cartoons to demonstrate acceptable and inappropriate reef visitor behavior. The author was involved in a research project designed to evaluate the success of a series of symbols in educating various reef visitor groups—particularly Japanese and Chinese visitors. Figure 7.1 contains some of the symbols that were evaluated.

The first stage in the research involved establishing existing levels of knowl-

Difficulty	Implications for Communicators
1. Smiling or laughing when confused or embarrassed. 2. Using bland facial expressions.	Australian communicators find it difficult to judge visitor responses.
3. Not keeping in place in queues. 4. Speaking loudly. 5. Bumping into others in a crowd.	Creates difficulties in managing larger groups.

Table 7.1: Some difficulties in Korean-Australian interaction

A. A Clear Symbol

Intended Message: Don't collect corals, rocks, or shells.

B. Two Confusing Symbols

Intended Message: Float a safe distance above the coral.

Intended Message: Don't litter or try to feed the fish.

Figure 7.1: Examples of symbols used to educate reef visitors

edge of appropriate behavior. While the study found that visitors generally had high levels of knowledge about what they should and should not do when visiting a coral reef environment, there were some significant differences. Japanese visitors, for example, were much less likely to be aware of the problems associated with throwing food scraps into the water or that shell collection was prohibited. Chinese visitors were more likely than others to believe that it was acceptable to stand on the coral.

The second stage involved investigating the impact of the symbols alone and the symbols with explanatory text on visitor knowledge. The results were not very positive. In most cases, neither the symbols alone nor the symbols and text had much of an impact, and where differences were found, it was often the case that the symbols and/or the text confused the visitors. Both clear and confusing symbols are given in Figure 7.1.

Another interesting outcome of the research was the reactions of reef tour staff to the results. Many expressed surprise at the relatively high levels of knowledge of appropriate behaviors, as this seemed to contradict their personal experiences of visitors behaving in damaging ways. One possible explanation is the human tendency to overestimate the extent of a problem based on a few extreme examples. Another possibility is that visitors may have the knowledge but still chose to behave inappropriately because of different levels of concern about the environment. This is consistent with Caro and Ewert's (1995) finding that visitors to California forests had lower levels of environmental concern if they were born outside the United States.

Visitor Knowledge

In several of the examples given in the previous section, it was noted that visitor characteristics such as experience, motivation, and culture influenced their responses to communication efforts through influencing existing knowledge. In the previous chapter, the importance of building upon existing knowledge was also stressed. Communicators need to know existing beliefs if they wish to change them, and communicators should know if visitors share the same understanding of the terms and concepts that might be used.

The author is currently involved in two projects which are directly concerned with understanding existing beliefs and knowledge of concepts and terms. The North Queensland region has two World Heritage Areas—the Great Barrier Reef and Wet Tropics Rainforests. Among the roles of the management agencies responsible for these areas are the presentation of the areas and their significant features to visitors, the encouragement of public support for the conservation of the areas, and the management of human behaviors that have negative impacts on the areas.

One particular problem has been a perceived lack of support among residents for the listing of these areas as World Heritage. Some managers suspected widespread misunderstanding of the World Heritage concept. In particular, it was thought that residents might be hostile because they believed World Heritage listing resulted in control over the area being given to non-Australian organizations. A 1,000-person telephone survey indicated that there was a substantial group of residents (30%) who believed that Australian governments did not have the power to control or manage World Heritage areas. In another survey of 370 people, a substantial number of residents and visitors were not sure who was responsible for the management of World Heritage areas (26%), who owned World Heritage areas (33%), or who decided what should be World Heritage (40%).

This second survey also asked visitors to read some statements about rainforests. The aim of this section was to identify potential problems in text proposed for a national parks visitor center. Table 7.2 contains the statements that were tested. Most of the text was understood by respondents. There were four exceptions:

1. Epiphytes. Twenty-six percent of those surveyed said they did not understand the word.
2. Melaleuca. Twenty-four percent of those surveyed said they did not understand the word.

Please read the following sentences and underline any words or phrases that you don't know or understand.

As you journey down the Cardwell Range, the major habitats of the Wet Tropics can be seen. Most of the Wet Tropics is covered by tropical rainforest, but bordering the rainforest are other important habitats such as open forest, *melaleuca* swamp, and mangroves.

The sudden transition from open forest to rainforest can be easily seen. Open forests, where eucalyptus and wattles grow, are drier, sunnier places, while rainforests are closed, shaded, humid places.

A layer of leaf litter can be found at the base of rainforests. Leaf litter comprises of fallen leaves, twigs, branches, bark and wood. Leaf litter breaks down to form humus, or decomposed vegetable matter.

Growing from the trunks of many rainforest trees are plants known as *epiphytes*. These plants can also grow from rocks. Epiphytes do not harm the host tree, or are not parasitic, as they do not penetrate the tree's living tissue.

The humid atmosphere inside the rainforest is caused largely by the great number of transpiring plants giving off water vapor and the absence of drying agents such as wind and bright sunlight.

The bark of rainforest trees is often colored and mottled by lichen. Lichen is made up of a green plant (algae) in partnership with a fungus.

Rainforests are characterized by a dense canopy where at least 70% of sunlight is blocked out.

Many rainforest trees are buttressed. *Buttress* roots appear as flattened, woody extensions which grow out from the base of the tree.

Rainforest trees have special rounded points called driptips. *Driptips* help the leaves shed moisture after rain.

Table 7.2: Proposed text for a national parks visitor center

3. Buttress. Sixteen percent did not understand the concept.
4. Driptips. Twelve percent did not understand the word.

These results clearly indicate some areas for further attention.

HOW CAN YOU GET TO KNOW VISITORS?

There are many ways to gather visitor information or to engage in evaluation. *Evaluation* can be defined simply as the collection of information to ensure that communication programs and activities are successful. A more formal definition states that evaluation is the "process of collecting and analyzing information about [an interpretive] program, or its impacts on an audience for the explicit purpose of improving its ability to serve the audience in the intended ways" (Ham, 1986, p. 9). It is important that all communicators have some understanding of evaluation. The aim of this chapter is to introduce communicators to evaluation.

Three Types of Visitor Evaluation

Front-end evaluation is about knowing who your audience is, where they come from, and what they expect. The research described in the first part of this chapter was all front-end evaluation.

Formative evaluation concerns what visitors already know and understand. If they already have a good understanding of World Heritage Values, they don't need a whole visitor center to tell them what these are. If they do not understand the concept of natural selection, then they will not understand evolution. Formative evaluation is much closer to the development of the specific communication strategies than front-end evaluation. Formative evaluation is much more targeted toward understanding how a specific interpretive activity will work. Formative evaluation can therefore also involve the testing of particular ideas for interpretation. Formative evaluation is when you test a mock-up of a map and see if visitors can use it before you print the final version.

Adams (1993) gives examples of both front-end and formative evaluation in the design of an African-American Exhibit at the Henry Ford Museum and Greenfield Village in Michigan. This indoor-outdoor historic museum planned to interpret a house in the village which had belonged to slaves in the 1840s and following years. Interviews with visitors to the museum were conducted to develop an understanding of what visitors would expect from the interpretation of this house and what they already knew about the period of history being interpreted. These surveys indicated a strong desire on the part of visitors to have African-American on-site interpreters. The surveys also indicated that visitors had many false conceptions about the lives of slaves. The next stage of the development and evaluation of the interpretation for this historic house involved the trailing of labels and audiotapes with samples of visitors to the outdoor museum. As a result of visitor responses, the tapes were shortened and the text modified. One tape was removed from the display as visitors indicated no understanding of its content.

The final and most common form of evaluation is **summative evaluation**. Summative evaluation involves examining and testing the effectiveness of interpretation that is already in place. It is also sometimes called *post hoc* evaluation because it occurs after the communication program has been designed and is up and running. Summative evaluation can tell managers whether or not objectives are being met and how a program should be changed and improved over time. Summative evaluation is about checking to see if your audience is getting your message. Summative evaluation is a necessary and important part of communication planning and management, but it has two major drawbacks. It is often difficult to use the results of summative evaluation because the interpretation is already in place. Formative and front-end evaluation have the advantage of being able to influence an interpretive activity before the resources involved in the activity have been committed. Summative evaluation has also often been used as a single product or study rather than serving an ongoing monitoring function. The key to the success of summative evaluation is being prepared to make changes to an existing interpretive activity if the results indicate that these are needed. It is also important to engage in ongoing monitoring because visitors change.

Some Evaluation Techniques
Unobtrusive Methods

There are several techniques which can provide information about visitors without having to directly approach the visitors. These are referred to as unobtrusive methods, and they include using counters, using trace measures, using archival information, and observing visitors.

Hall and McArthur (1993) list a variety of different types of counters and places where they can be used. Counters primarily provide an indication of the level of use of different areas or interpretive programs. Level of use can be important in determining the popularity of different places and activities and for highlighting potential problems in terms of crowding and other negative impacts. The limitation of counters is that they point to what might be popular or problematic, but provide no information on why a place is popular or how to manage impacts.

Trace measures include assessments of physical impacts on site by such things as litter, vandalism, and erosion. As with counters, such measures can highlight potential and actual problems for management, but do not provide any information for developing solutions. Other trace measures include recording the questions visitors ask of staff. This can provide information on the areas that might require further interpretation. Similar methods include keeping records on what books, posters, and materials visitors purchase. This provides some insight into what visitors have found to be the interesting or outstanding places, features, or topics of their experience. With the rise of computer technology, it is common to find information or quiz computer programs in tourist and recreation settings. A useful addition to such programs is the capacity to record the kind of information requested by visitors or how they answer quiz questions.

Observation

The main unobtrusive technique used in evaluation research is observation. There are three main types of observation study: targeted, tracking, and behavioral mapping. *Targeted observation* studies collect information about visitors and their behavior at a specific or targeted point or place. Such a target for observation may be a single exhibit in a visitor center or museum, or a sign on a self-guided trail. This technique allows for detailed data to be collected about this specific feature, but does not provide information about how this target feature relates to other features (in our example, other exhibits or signs) in the larger setting. *Tracking studies* involve following visitors through an entire setting, for example, a gallery of a museum or along a complete self-guided trail or walk. This is a very common technique, but it can be difficult to collect reliable data if the setting is large or crowded. It can also be very expensive in terms of time in large settings. Finally, *behavioral mapping* refers to the technique of entering a setting, such as a visitor center or picnic ground, at regular intervals and recording what is happening at that point. This can be a very efficient technique for large areas.

Observations, regardless of the techniques used, can record very valuable information about visitors and their behavior. Observations can tell us what features attract visitor attention and how long they hold that attention. Observations can also tell us something about our visitors, such as their sex, estimated age, and whom they are with. Observations can also tell us what visitors do. Do they touch vegetation? Do they stay on the path? Do they use the map or put it in their pockets?

What observation cannot tell us is why visitors touch the tree, why they spend so long at a sign, or why they put the map in their pocket. To find out the answers to these questions, we need to ask the visitors.

Surveys

A survey can be defined as

a method of collecting information about a human population in which direct contact is made with the units of the study (individuals, organizations, communities, etc.) through such systematic means as questionnaires and interview schedules. (Warwick and Lininger, 1975, pp. 1-2)

There are several different types of surveys, and these differ on one key feature. This key feature is how much contact there is between the visitor and the researchers. Surveys can range from interviews which have direct, face-to-face contact with the visitor, to mail surveys which have very limited contact with the visitor. In general, the less the contact between researchers and visitors, the harder it is to get visitors to complete the survey. Kraus and Allen (1987) suggest that response rates of 50 to 60 percent are acceptable; however, they suggest several techniques for improving response rates. These include keeping the survey as short as possible, giving clear instructions and a reason for the study, making sure the survey form is attractive and professionally set out, and using follow-up notes and reminders. Offering benefits for participation is another method for encouraging participation.

The key to all surveys is the nature of the questions asked. These can range from unstructured or open-ended questions to forced-choice, structured questions. Figure 7.2 gives examples of questions which differ in their degree of structure. This figure provides only a few examples of the many ways in which questions can be organized. In general, the more open and unstructured a question is, the broader the range of potential responses and the more difficult it is to answer. In other words, open-ended questions in principle should result in detailed answers, but in practice, this is rarely the case. Another problem with open-ended, unstructured questions is how to code the replies. It is not easy to summarize unstructured answers. At the other end of the scale, however, very structured questions have several limitations. At their most extreme, structured questions may simply not be very informative because they are too restricted. In particular, it is important in struc-

Goal: To understand visitor motives.

Why did you come to the park?
_____
_____

Why did you come to the park?
(Please tick as many as appropriate.)

_____ to enjoy a day out with family and friends
_____ to experience nature
_____ to be by myself
_____ to engage in a specific activity
_____ to learn about the park
_____ other (please tell us)

_____
_____

Why did you come to the park?
(Please tick one answer only.)
_____ to enjoy a day out with family and friends
_____ to experience nature
_____ to be by myself
_____ to engage in a specific activity
_____ to learn about the park
_____ other (please tell us)

_____
_____

Why did you come to the park?
(Please tick one answer only.)
_____ to enjoy a day out with family and friends
_____ to experience nature
_____ to be by myself
_____ to engage in a specific activity

Did you come to experience nature?
                    _____ Yes
                    _____ No

Very unstructured

Very structured

Figure 7.2: Questions varying in structure

tured questions that the researcher has included all potential answers. For example, if you want to know about the activities that park visitors are interested in and you want to use a checklist, you must ensure that all the major or important activities are included on that list. Figure 7.3 contains some more examples of survey questions.

Focus Groups

A focus group is where a small number of people, usually eight to 12, are brought together with a moderator to discuss in detail some topic of interest to the researcher or evaluator (Churchill, 1991). The moderator usually leads the discussion and follows a loose set of questions. The focus-group members then usually talk about the ideas or questions and about each other's responses for two to three hours. The use of focus groups is an exploratory research technique. It has been noted that focus groups are often seen as an alternative to surveys in evaluation research (Churchill, 1991). This is a serious error. Focus groups are designed to generate ideas and provide information to researchers about issues and topics that have not been previously examined. For example, a focus group might be used to generate ideas about how to present a certain topic to visitors. Or if a researcher wants to know about visitor motivations in a setting and there is no previous or relevant research to use in the design of survey questions, then a focus group might be helpful in suggesting directions to take. But, as Churchill (1991, p. 142) warns, it is

> very easy to forget that the discussion, and consequently the results, are greatly influenced by the moderator and the specific directions he or she provides.... One has to remember that results are not representative of what would be found in the general population and are thus **not** projectable.... Focus groups should **not** be used, therefore, to develop head counts of the proportion of people who feel a particular way. Focus groups are better for generating ideas and insights than for systematically examining them.

In other words, a focus group might be useful in identifying a range of problems with a communication program, but a survey is necessary to determine which are the most important and most common. Focus groups do not represent all visitors.

SUMMARY

Getting to know your visitors can help make personal connections to them by providing familiar examples or using topics of interest.

Getting to know your visitors can also help in the planning of content by telling you what they already know or understand.

Some important pieces of visitor information are:
- what visitors know and understand,

Rating Scales

How interested are you in learning about tropical rainforests?

| Not at all | | | | | | | | | Very |
| Interested | | | | | | | | | Interested |

0   1   2   3   4   5   6   7   8   9   0

Ranking

How interested are you in the following topics? Please rank them all from 1, most interested, to 5, least interested.

- ☐ Animals in the region
- ☐ European history of the region
- ☐ Aboriginal history of the region
- ☐ Birds in the region
- ☐ Plants in the region

Check lists

Please tick five words from the following list that best describe the Great Barrier Reef.

- ☐ Beautiful　　　　☐ Scary
- ☐ Fragile　　　　　☐ Big
- ☐ Living　　　　　☐ Peaceful
- ☐ Valuable　　　　☐ Wilderness
- ☐ Unique　　　　　☐ Important

Underlining key information*

Please read this story and <u>underline</u> anything that you would do differently from the text.

> He kept mostly to the track, except when he saw a good shortcut. Sometimes he got a lift to the beach with his campsite neighbors who had a four-wheel drive. He liked that, especially when they went down a track marked "Revegetation area" which took them onto an uncrowded beach.

Judging scenarios**

Scenario Wetlands development

A number of major tourist complexes have been proposed on and immediately adjacent to a large mangrove/wetland area near the city. These mangrove/wetlands are environmentally sensitive and are the habitat of many animals, fish, and birds. However, the tourist developments may bring many tourists and a number of jobs to the area. What would you like to see happen?

A. Allow no development near the wetlands and encourage developers to build in less sensitive areas.
B. Permit only a few developments near the wetlands and monitor the extent of the impacts.
C. Allow tourist developments to proceed and encourage developers to set aside a portion of the wetlands and build an observatory/interpretation centre for tourists to see some of the wildlife.

*　　Source: McArthur & Hall, 1993, p.263.
**　　Source: Pearce, Moscardo & Ross, 1991.

Figure 7.3: Types of survey questions

- what their expectations and motives are, and
- whom they are with.

We can also involve visitors by getting them to evaluate the communication programs provided.

Evaluation can involve:

- observing visitors and how they respond to communication efforts, or
- asking visitors for their reactions, thoughts, and suggestions by using interviews, surveys, or focus groups.

■ 8

Coming to Conclusions

THROUGHOUT THIS BOOK, I have suggested that readers think of themselves as travelers or explorers. I have done this for several reasons. Firstly, one way to encourage mindfulness is to try and take the perspective of others. So it seemed appropriate to encourage the reader to take the perspective of a visitor. Secondly, I have proposed the use of themes as a way to organize content. Finally, it was an effort to add a little fun. In keeping with our metaphor of ourselves as travelers, this chapter will bring us to the end of the journey.

SOME POINTS TO PONDER

Before we reach the end of our journey, there are several short but important diversions that are worthy of our attention.

Difficult Topics

Pearce (1982b) provides some examples of travel stories about challenging experiences. For example,

> My overriding experience in Manila was the sight of thousands of human beings living in cardboard boxes, open fields, trash cans, and on the streets within 100 yards of glass-studded white walls enclosing some of the most beautiful private and government-owned residences in the world. I was distressed and felt totally helpless in the face of the thousands of people locked in a seemingly hopeless situation. Had I been willing to give them everything I possessed in life I would have done very little for very few for a very short time.
>
> (Pearce, 1982b, p. 128)

and

> I walked into the Basilica and was overcome by the simple beauty and inspiring atmosphere of the church. I had recently seen many of the world's

most famous, but none impressed me so much. I am not a religious person at all but I found myself sitting in a pew thinking of many religious ideals and suddenly found I was praying—more desperately than I thought I ever could or knew how to. And then I started crying. It seemed endless but I experienced relief with some answers in finding myself.

(Pearce, 1982b, pp. 131-132)

The first example is clearly a negative experience. The story implies, however, that it was more than simply frustrating or annoying; the experience made quite an impact on the traveler and his world view. In a similar fashion, the second story is also of an experience that had a profound impact on the traveler. Stories such as these contradict a not uncommon view of tourism and recreation as primarily superficial entertainment (see Smith and Godbey, 1991; and Moscardo, 1992, for further discussion of this point).

Many popular places for tourism and recreation are sites associated with more challenging topics. These include battlefields and prisoner-of-war camps, presentations of natural disasters, presentations of war and other memorials, and presentations of cultural conflict.

Difficult topics can arise in any tourist place with a human history. Such topics are not easy to present. Uzzell (1989) has suggested that such topics are often avoided by communicators. This reflects the view that visitors may not wish to be presented with difficult topics while they are on holidays or at leisure. Uzzell goes on to argue that this view is misguided, and that so-called "hot" topics can actually be used by communicators to create challenging experiences and to make strong connections. Machlis (1992) provides a similar analysis of the interpretation of war in United States National Parks.

Lacey (1995) provides an example of the importance of presenting controversy in his description of the development of the Tower Museum in Derry City, Northern Ireland. The communicators here had to decide on how to present the recent history of the city, which has been very much in the center of the conflict over Irish independence. He notes that "it is our experience that most of the visitors who come here actually want to know what is going on" (p. 18). The communicators at the Tjapukai Aboriginal Cultural Park in Cairns, Australia, were faced with a dilemma similar to that of the designers of the Tower Museum. How much attention should they pay to recent history and conflict? Their decision was to present the difficulties and the conflict to the visitors. Again, the visitors have been supportive, with high satisfaction reported for the History Theatre, which presents a graphic audiovisual of European treatment of Aboriginal people (Pearce et al., 1997).

Clearly, in many places, visitors seek and appreciate information on difficult topics. Uzzell (1989) goes further and argues that difficult topics present an opportunity to generate an emotional response from visitors that can result in a greater impact from your communication. One of the author's doctoral studies conducted at the Australian War Memorial in Canberra supports this argument. Specifically, the author observed and surveyed visitors in two galleries—one presenting the Gallipoli campaign, and one presenting the conflict in the Sinai/Palestine areas. Both campaigns were in World War I. The Gallipoli campaign has a much higher profile for the Australian public and has been strongly associated in the media with concepts of Australian courage and loyalty and the futility of war. This higher profile was confirmed in a pilot test, where it was found that people rated the Gallipoli campaign as the most important and familiar episode in Australia's military history. Visitors also reported higher levels of feelings of sadness, anger, pride, respect, despair, and regret in the Gallipoli gallery. These feelings were found to be significantly related to mindfulness. In other words, an emotional response was associated with mindfulness.

Making Sure Communication Is Sustainable

The major argument for having effective visitor communication programs and activities is that they can create and support sustainable tourism and recreation. An important message in many settings will be how to minimize negative environmental impacts. It is therefore important that communicators think about the potential impacts of such things as trails, signs, and visitor centers.

Staff at the visitor center at Cradle Mountain National Park (Tasmania, Australia) identified a number of problems in the design of the center, including several related to its ecological sustainability (Moscardo, 1993b). Specifically, the center was heated primarily by a large, open wood fire. This fire was certainly attractive, but was not very energy efficient. Also, the lighting was designed so that all lights came on, even if lighting was only needed for one area. Clearly some environmental-impact assessment procedure for the design of visitor facilities would be a valuable activity.

THE WHOLE THING IN A NUTSHELL

We have now come to the end of our journey, but I would like to keep the travel metaphor for a little bit longer. Particularly, I would like to present the key arguments, points, and principles as a set of slides which provide the highlights of this journey.

Slide 1: Why Did We Begin This Journey?

- to look for ways to make tourism and recreation more sustainable.
- sustainable tourism and recreation provide a quality experience for visitors, improve the quality of life of host communities, and protect the quality of the environment.
- good communication or interpretation can contribute to sustainable tourism and recreation through enhancing the quality of the experience for visitors and assisting the management of visitors and their impacts.

Slide 2: How Can Communication Help?
- good communication can enhance visitor experiences by providing information on alternatives and options, encouraging safety and comfort, and by being a core element of the actual experience.
- good communication can assist in managing visitors by influencing where they go and informing them about appropriate behaviors.
- good communication creates mindful visitors.

Slide 3: What Is a Mindful Visitor?
- a mindful visitor actively processes new information, creates new categories for information, and thinks about new ways to behave.
- mindfulness is associated with more learning, better decision making, increased self-esteem, and feelings of control and enjoyment.

Slide 4: A Mindfulness Model

Varied, multisensory, novel approaches which give visitors control and make personal connections and which have a good orientation system

Combined with visitor interest in content

|

Create mindful visitors

|

If the communication has a clear structure matched to what visitors know,

|

then learning, understanding and satisfaction should result

Slide 5: The Basic Principles for Effective Communication
1. Help visitors find their way around.
2. Make connections to visitors and get them involved.
3. Provide variety.
4. Tell a good story that makes sense.
5. Know and respect visitors.

Slide 6: How Can We Help Visitors Find Their Way Around?

- by designing complete and consistent systems which include directional signs, "you-are-here" maps, hand-held maps, and physical cues
- maps are particularly important

Good maps should
- highlight distinctive landmarks
- highlight major pathways
- include realistic symbols
- be aligned to match the visitor's perspective
- put text on the map rather than beside it
- use some color
- be simple

Slide 7: How Can We Connect to Visitors?

We can
- engage them in conversations,
- use analogies and metaphors from their everyday lives,
- tell stories with characters they can relate to, and
- choose topics within everyday experience.

We can also give visitors some control by
- offering them choices,
- asking them questions, and
- encouraging them to participate in the communication.

Slide 8: Providing Varied Experiences

Variety is a key element in encouraging mindfulness. We can vary:
- the senses required,
- the social nature of the experience,
- the level of physical activity required,
- the level of mental activity required, and
- the media used.

Slide 9: Telling a Good Story That Makes Sense

Visitors prefer:
- to be told stories, and
- to have the relationships between pieces of information made clear.

Visitors don't like information presented as isolated facts.

Visitors can only make sense of new information if they can connect it to something they already know.

Slide 10: Ideas to Help Visitors Understand

Communicators can
- provide advance organizers or instructions to help visitors understand how information is organized,
- use themes to link information, and
- tell stories.

Slide 11: Getting to Know Your Visitors

Communicators need to get to know their visitors.

In particular, it would be useful to know
- how much experience of the place or activity visitors have,
- why they are visiting,
- who they are with,
- their cultural background, and what they already know.

Communicators can also evaluate their efforts by observing visitor reactions or asking visitors for comments and suggestions.

All that is left to say is thank you for the time spent reading this book and good luck with your communication programs.

■ References

Abrahamson, D., Gennaro, E., & Heller, P. (1983). Animal exhibits: A naturalistic study. *Roundtable Reports, 8*(2), 6-9.

Adams, G.D. (1993). Using research to guide the development of an African American exhibit. In D. Thompson, A. Benefield, S. Bitgood, H. Shettel, & R. Williams (Eds.), *Visitor Studies: Theory, Research and Practice* (Vol. 5), (pp. 136–142). Jacksonville, AL: Visitor Studies Association.

Ajzen, I. (1992). Persuasive communication theory in social psychology. In M.J. Manfredo (Ed.), *Influencing human behavior* (pp. 1-28). Champaign, IL: Sagamore Publishing.

Alderson, W.T., & Low, S.P. (1985). Interpretation of historic sites, Nashville, TN: American Association for State and Local History. In D.M. Knudson, T.T. Cable, & L. Beck (1995), *Interpretation of cultural and natural resources.* State College, PA: Venture.

Alexander, C.N., Langer, G.J., Newman, R.I., Chandler, H.M., & Davies, J.L. (1989). Transcendental meditation, mindfulness, and longevity. *Journal of Personality and Social Psychology, 57*, 950-964.

Almagor, V. (1985). A tourist's "Vision quest" in an African game reserve. *Annals of Tourism Research, 12*(1), 31-48.

Alt, M.B., & Shaw, K.M. (1984). Characteristics of ideal museum exhibits. *British Journal of Psychology, 75*, 25-36.

Anonymous. (1996). *Presentation and publication for telling your story.* (On-line) http://www.oii.org/presonline.html.

Anooshian, L.J. (1996). Diversity within spatial cognition: Strategies underlying spatial knowledge. *Environment and Behavior, 28*(4), 471-493.

Anooshian, L.J., & Siebert, P.S. (1996). Diversity within spatial cognition. *Applied Cognitive Psychology, 10*, 281-299.

Arndt, M.A., Screven, C., Benusa, D., & Bishop, T. (1992). Behavior and learning in a zoo environment under different signage conditions. *Visitor Studies: Theory, Research and Practice, 5*, 245-251.

Balling, J.D., & Falk, J.H. (1980). A perspective on field trips: Environmental effects on learning. *Curator, 23*, 229-240.

Bechtel, R.B. (1967). Hodometer research in museums. *Museum News, 45*(7), 23-26.

Beeho, A.J., & Prentice, R.C. (1995). Evaluating the experiences and benefits gained by tourists visiting a socio-industrial heritage museum. *Museum Management and Curatorship, 14*(3), 229-251.

Birney, B.A. (1988). Brookfield Zoo's "Flying Walk" exhibit. Formative evaluation aids in the development of an interactive exhibit in an informal learning setting. *Environment and Behavior, 20,* 416-434.

Bitgood, S. (1987). When is a zoo like a city? *Visitor Behavior, 1*(4), 5.

Bitgood, S. (1988). Museum "fatigue": Early studies. *Visitor Behavior, 3*(1), 4-5.

Bitgood, S., & Patterson, D. (1987a). Orientation and wayfinding in a small museum. *Visitor Behavior, 1*(4), 6.

Bitgood, S., & Patterson, D. (1987b). Principles of orientation and circulation. *Visitor Behavior, 1*(4), 4.

Bitgood, S., & Richardson, K. (1987). Wayfinding at the Birmingham Zoo. *Visitor Behavior, 1*(4), 9.

Bitgood, S., Benefield, A., Patterson, D., & Litwak, H. (1990). Influencing visitor attention. *Visitor Studies: Theory, Research and Practice, 3,* 221-230.

Bitgood, S., Hines, J., Hamberger, W., & Ford, W. (1991). Visitor circulation through a changing gallery. *Visitor Studies: Theory, Research and Practice, 4,* 103-114.

Bitgood, S., Patterson, D., & Benefield, A. (1988). Exhibit design and visitor behavior: Empirical relationships. *Environment and Behavior, 20,* 474-491.

Bitgood, S., Patterson, D., & Nichols, G. (1986). *Report of a survey of visitors to the Anniston Museum of Natural History.* (Technical Report No. 86-50.) Jacksonville, AL: Psychology Institute, Jacksonville State University.

Black, N., & Pearce, P.L. (1995). Maps for tourists: An exploration of function and form. In *Tourism Research and Education in Australia.* Proceedings from the Tourism and Educators Conference, Gold Coast (1994). Canberra, Australia: Bureau of Tourism Research.

Blades, M., & Medlicott, L. (1992). Developmental differences in the ability to give route directions from a map. *Journal of Environmental Psychology, 12,* 175-185.

Blud, L.M. (1990). Social interaction and learning among family groups visiting a museum. *Museum Management and Curatorship, 9,* 43-51.

Borun, M. (1977). *Measuring the immeasurable: A pilot study of museum effectiveness.* Washington, D.C.: Association of Science Technology Centers.

Borun, M. (1991). Confronting naive notions through interactive exhibits. In *Doing time: Museums, education and accountability.* Proceedings of 1991 Museum Education Association of Australia Conference, Sydney.

Borun, M., & Adams, K.A. (1991). From hands on to minds on. *Visitor Studies: Theory, Research and Practice, 4,* 115-120.

Borun, M., Massey, C., & Lutter, T. (1993). Naive knowledge and the design of science museum exhibits. *Curator, 36*(3), 201-219.

Bramwell, B., & Lane, B. (1993). Sustainable tourism: An evolving global approach. *Journal of Sustainable Tourism, 1*(1), 1-5.

Bransford, J.D., & Johnson, M.K. (1973). Consideration of some problems in comprehension. In W.G. Chase (Ed.), *Visual information processing* (pp. 383-438). New York: Academic Press.

Brockmeyer, F.M., Bowman, M.L., & Mullins, G. (1983). Sensory versus non-sensory interpretation: A study of senior citizens' preferences. *Journal of Environmental Education, 14*, 3-7.

Brown, B.J., Hanson, M.E., Liverman, D.M., & Merideth, R.W., Jr. (1987). Global sustainability: Toward definition. *Environmental Management, 11*, 713-719.

Brown, C. (1995). Making the most of family visits. *Museum Management and Curatorship, 14*(1), 65-71.

Bruntland, G.H. (1987). *The Bruntland Report. Our common future.* World Commission on Environment and Development. Oxford, UK: Oxford University Press.

Butler, B.H., & Sussman, M.B. (1989). *Museum visits and activities for family life enrichment.* New York: Haworth Press.

Butler, D.L., Acquino, A.L., Hissong, A.A., & Scott, P.A. (1993). Wayfinding by newcomers in a complex building. *Human Factors, 35*(1), 159-173.

Caro, V., & Ewert, A. (1995). The influence of acculturation on environmental concerns. *Journal of Environmental Education, 26*(3), 13-21.

Cave, J., & Wolf, R.L. (1983). *Don't brush your teeth anymore. Toothpaste's got earth in it! A study of the role that objects can play in the experience of visitors to a museum.* Washington DC: Smithsonian Institution, Office of Museum Programs Evaluation Studies.

Chaiken, S., & Stangor, C. (1987). Attitudes and attitude change. *Annual Review of Psychology, 38*, 575-630.

Chambers, M. (1984). Is anyone out there? *Museum News, 62*(5), 47-54.

Chanowitz, B., & Langer, E. (1981). Knowing more (or less) than you can show: Understanding control through the mindlessness/mindfulness distinction. In M.E.P. Seligman & J. Barber (Eds.), *Human helplessness.* New York: Academic Press.

Chown, E., Kaplan, S., & Kortenkamp, D. (1995). Prototypes, location, and associative networks (PLAN): Toward a unified theory of cognitive mapping. *Cognitive Science, 19*, 1-51.

Churchill, G.A., Jr. (1991). *Marketing research: Methodological foundations* (5th ed.). Chicago: Dryden Press.

Cohen, M.S., Winkel, G.H., Olsen, R., & Wheeler, F. (1977). Orientation in a museum: An experimental visitor study. *Curator, 20*(2), 85-107.

Coleman, C. (1997). Tourist traffic in English national parks: An innovative approach to management. *Journal of Tourism Studies, 8*(1), 2-15.

Cornell, E.H., Heth, C.D., & Alberts, D.M. (1994). Place recognition and wayfinding by children and adults. *Memory and Cognition, 22*(6), 633-643.

Davidson, B., Heald, C.L., & Hein, G.E. (1991). Increased exhibit accessibility through multisensory interaction. *Curator, 34*(4), 273-290.

Devlin, A.S., & Bernstein, J. (1995). Interactive wayfinding. *Journal of Environmental Psychology, 15,* 23-38.

Diamond, J. (1986). The behavior of family groups in science museums. *Curator, 29*(2), 139-154.

Diamond, J., Smith, A., & Bond, A. (1988). California Academy of Sciences discovery room. *Curator, 31,* 157-166.

Dobbs, S.M. (1990). Silent pedagogy in art museums. *Curator, 33*(3), 217-235.

Dowell, D.L., & McCool, S.F. (1986). Evaluation of a wilderness information dissemination program. In *Proceedings: National Wilderness Conference* (pp. 494-500), Fort Collins, Colorado.

Driver, B.L., Brown, P.J., Stankey, G.H., & Gregoire, T.G. (1987). The ROS planning system: Evolution, basic concepts, and research needed. *Leisure Sciences, 9,* 201-212.

Edwards, R.W., Loomis, R.J., Fusco, M.E., & McDermott, M. (1990). Motivation and information needs of art museum visitors: A cluster analytic study. *ILVS Review, 1*(2), 20-35.

Edwards, Y. (1979). *The land speaks: Organizing and running an interpretation system.* Toronto: The National and Provincial Parks Association of Canada.

ESD Working Group (1991). *Tourism: Final report.* Canberra: Australian Government Publishing Service.

Falk, J.H. (1983). A cross-cultural investigation of the novel field trip phenomenon: National Museum of Natural History, New Delhi. *Curator, 26,* 315-323.

Falk, J.H. (1991). Analysis of the behavior of family visitors in natural history museums. *Curator, 34*(1), 44-57.

Falk, J.H. (1995). Factors influencing African American leisure time utilization of museums. *Journal of Leisure Research, 27*(1), 41-60.

Falk, J.H., Phillips, K.E., & Boxer, J.J. (1992). Invisible Forces Exhibition. *Visitor Studies: Theory, Research and Practice, 5,* 211-226.

Fazio, R.H. (1979). Information and education techniques to improve minimum impacts use. Knowledge in wilderness areas. In R. Ihner (Ed.), *Recreational impacts on wildlands conference proceedings* (pp. 227-233). Seattle, WA: U.S. Department of Agriculture Forest Service.

Fazio, R.H., Powell, M.C., & Herr, P.M. (1983). Toward a process model of the attitude-behavior relation. *Journal of Personality and Social Psychology, 44,* 723-735.

Fine, E.C., & Speer, J.H. (1985). Tour guide performances as sight serialization. *Annals of Tourism Research, 12,* 73-96.

Flemming. (1996). *Story telling.* (Online) http://www.worldtrans.org/ nen/ stprytelling.html.

Foster, J.S., Koran, J.J., Jr., Koran, M.L., Stark, S., Blackwood, A., & Landers, H. (1988). The effect of multispecies exhibits on visitor attention at the Jacksonville Zoological Park. *Visitor Studies: Theory, Research and Practice, 1,* 113-119.

Frack, S. (1996). *Telling the story of a rock.* (Online) http:// nesen.unl.edu/activities/geology/storyrock.html.

Fraser, K. (1991). *Bad trips.* New York: Vintage Departures.

Gallagher, J. (1983). *Visiting historic gardens.* Leeds, UK: School of Planning and Environmental Studies, Leeds Polytechnic.

Gallup, T.P. (1981). *The effectiveness of a cartoon illustrated interpretive brochure on the enhancement of campers' knowledge of rules and the decrease in rates of rule violation per campsite.* Master's thesis, the Pennsylvania State University.

Garland, H., Haynes, J., & Grubb, G. (1979). Transit map color coding and street detail. *Environment and Behavior, 11,* 162-184.

Gennaro, G.D. (1981). The effectiveness of using pre-visit instructional materials on learning from a museum field trip experience. *Journal of Research in Science Teaching, 18*(3), 275-279.

Gennaro, G.D., Stoneberg, S.A., & Tanck, S. (1984). Chance or the prepared mind? In S. Nichols (Ed.), *Museum education anthology 1973-1983* (pp. 201-205). Washington, DC: Museum Education Roundtable.

Gerber, R. (1984). Factors affecting the competence and performance in map language for children at the concrete level of map reasoning. *Cartography, 13*(3), 205-213.

Geva, A., & Goldman, A. (1991). Satisfaction measurement in guided tours. *Annals of Tourism Research, 18*(2), 177-185.

Gillies, P., & Wilson, R. (1982). Participatory exhibits: Is fun educational? *Museums Journal, 82,* 131-135.

Glicksohn, J. (1994). Rotation, orientation, and cognitive mapping. *American Journal of Psychology, 107*(1), 39-51.

Golledge, R.G., Dougherty, V., & Bell, S. (1995). Acquiring spatial knowledge. *Annals of the Association of American Geographers, 85*(1), 134-158.

Gopal, S., Klatzky, R.L., & Smith, T.R. (1989). Navigator: A psychologically based model of environmental learning through navigation. *Journal of Environmental Psychology, 9,* 309-331.

Griggs, S. (1982). Formative evaluation of exhibits at the British Museum (Natural History). *Curator, 24*(3), 189-201.

Guy, B.S., Curtis, W.W., & Crotts, J.C. (1990). Environmental learning of first-time travelers. *Annals of Tourism Research, 17*(3), 419-431.

Hall, C.M., & McArthur, S. (1993). Heritage management: An introductory framework. In C.M. Hall & S. McArthur (Eds.), *Heritage management in New Zealand and Australia* (pp. 1-17). Auckland, New Zealand: Oxford University Press.

Ham, S.H. (1986). Evaluation and interpretation. In G.E. Machlis (Ed.), *Interpretive views* (pp. 9-38). Washington, DC: National Parks and Conservation Association.

Healy, V.C. (1989). The effects of advance organizer and prerequisite knowledge passages on the learning and retention of science concepts. *Journal of Research in Science Teaching, 26*(7), 627-642.

Hicks, E.C. (1986). An artful science. *Museum News, 64*(3), 32-39.

Hilke, D.D. (1989). The family as a learning system: An observational study of families in museums. In B.H. Butler & M.B. Sussman (Eds.), *Museum visits and activities for family life enrichment* (pp. 101-129). New York: Haworth Press.

Hilke, D.D., Hennings, E.C., & Springuel, M. (1988). The impact of interactive computer software on visitors' experiences: A case study. *ILVS Review, 1*(1), 34-49.

Hirschi, K.D., & Screven, C.G. (1988). Effects of questions on visitor reading behavior. *ILVS Review, 1*(1), 50-61.

Holding, C.S. (1994). Further evidence for the hierarchical representation of spatial information. *Journal of Environmental Psychology, 14*, 137-147.

Hood, M.G. (1989). Leisure criteria of family participation and nonparticipation in museums. In B.H. Butler, & M.B. Sussman (Eds.), *Museum visits and activities for family life enrichment* (pp. 151-169). New York: Haworth Press.

Horn, A.L. (1980). A comparative study of two methods of conducting docent tours in art museums. *Curator, 23*, 105-117.

Huffman, M.G., & Williams, D.R. (1987). The use of microcomputers for park trail information dissemination. *Journal of Park and Recreation Administration, 5*, 34-46.

Hultsman, W.Z. (1988). Applications of a touch-sensitive computer in park settings. *Journal of Park and Recreation Administration, 6*(1), 1-11.

Inskeep, E. (1991). *Tourism planning: An integrated and sustainable development approach.* New York: Van Nostrand Reinhold.

Jacobson, S.K. (1988). Media effectiveness in a Malaysian park system. *Journal of Environmental Education, 19*(4), 22-27.

Jafari, J. (1990). Research and scholarship: The basis of tourism education. *Journal of Tourism Studies, 1*(1), 33-41.

Kanel, J., & Tamir, P. (1991). Different labels—different learnings. *Curator, 34*(1), 18-30.

Kaplan, S., & Kaplan, R. (1982). *Cognition and environment.* New York: Praeger.

Keates, J.S. (1982). *Understanding maps.* London: Longman.

Keillor, G. (1985). *Lake Wobegone days.* London: Faber.

Kim, E.J. (1996). *Korean tourists' cross-cultural experiences in Australia.* Paper presented at the Travel and Tourism Research Association Conference, Las Vegas, Nevada.

Kirasic, K.C., & Mathes, E.A. (1990). Effects of different means for conveying environmental information on elderly adults' spatial cognition and behavior. *Environment and Behavior, 22*(5), 591-607.

Kitchin, R.M. (1994). Cognitive maps. *Journal of Environmental Psychology, 14*, 1-19.

Kitchin, R.M. (1996). Increasing the integrity of cognitive mapping research. *Progress in Human Geography, 20*(1), 56-84.

Kitchin, R.M., Blades, M., & Golledge, R.G. (1997). Understanding spatial concepts at the geographic scale without the use of vision. *Progress in Human Geography, 21*(2), 225-242.

Klevans, M. (1990). Evaluation of interactive microcomputers. *Visitor Studies: Theory, Research and Practice, 3,* 237-255.

Knudson, D.M., Cable, T.T., & Beck, L. (1995). *Interpretation of cultural and natural resources.* State College, PA: Venture.

Koran, J.J., Jr., Longino, S.J., & Shafer, L.D. (1983a). A framework for conceptualizing research in natural history museums and science centres. *Journal of Research in Science Teaching, 20,* 325-339.

Koran, J.J., Jr., Shafer, L.D., & Koran, M.L. (1983b). The relative effects of pre- and post-attention directing devices on learning from a "walk through" museum exhibit. *Journal of Research in Science Teaching, 20*(4), 341-364.

Koran, Jr., J.J., Koran, M.L., & Foster, J.S. (1989). The potential contributions of cognitive psychology to visitor studies. *Visitor Studies: Theory, Research and Practice, 2,* 72-79.

Koran, J.J., Jr., Morrison, L., Lehman, J.R., Koran, M.L., & Gandara, L. (1984). Attention and curiosity in museums. *Journal of Research in Science Teaching, 21,* 357-363.

Korenic, M.S. (1991). The rainforest in Milwaukee. *Curator, 34*(2), 144-160.

Korn, R. (1988). Self-guiding brochures: An evaluation. *Curator, 31,* 9-19.

Kotler, P., Bowen, J., & Makens, J. (1996). *Marketing for hospitality and tourism.* Upper Saddle River, NJ: Prentice Hall.

Kraus, R., & Allen, L. (1987). *Research and evaluation in recreation, parks and leisure studies.* Columbus, OH: Publishing Horizons.

Krippendorf, J. (1987). *The holiday makers: Understanding the impact of leisure and travel.* London: William Heinemann.

Kulhavy, R.W., & Stock, W.A. (1996). How cognitive maps are learned and remembered. *Annals of the Association of American Geographers, 86*(1), 123-145.

Lacey, B. (1995). The Tower Museum, Derry. *Interpretation, 1*(1), 17-19.

Laetsch, W.M., Diamond, J., Gottfried, J.L., & Rosenfeld, S. (1980). Children and family groups in science centers. *Science and Children, 7*(6), 14-17.

Lane, B. (1991). Sustainable tourism: A new concept for the interpreter. *Interpretation Journal No. 49,* 1-4.

Langer, E. (1989). *Mindfulness.* Reading, MA: Addison-Wesley.

Langer, E., & Abelson, R. (1974). A patient by any other name...: Clinician group differences in labelling bias. *Journal of Consulting and Clinical Psychology, 42,* 4-9.

Langer, E., & Newman, H. (1979). The role of mindlessness in a typical social psychology experiment. *Personality and Social Psychology Bulletin, 5,* 295-299.

Langer, E., & Rodin, J. (1976). The effects of enhanced personal responsibility for the aged: A field experiment in an institutional setting. *Journal of Personality and Social Psychology, 34,* 191-198.

Langer, E.J., Bashner, R.S., and Chanowitz, B. (1985). Decreasing prejudice by increasing discrimination. *Journal of Personality and Social Psychology, 49*, 113-120.

Lawton, C.A. (1996). Strategies for indoor wayfinding. *Journal of Environmental Psychology, 16*, 137-145.

Lawton, C.A., Charleston, S.I., & Zieles, A.S. (1996). Individual- and gender-related differences in indoor wayfinding. *Environment and Behavior, 28*(2), 204-219.

Lee, O., Fradd, S.H., & Sutman, F.X. (1995). Science knowledge and cognitive strategy use among culturally and linguistically diverse students. *Journal of Research in Science Teaching, 32*(8), 797-816.

Lehman, J.R., & Lehman, K.M. (1984). The relative effects of experimenter and subject generated questions on learning from museum case exhibits. *Journal of Research in Science Teaching, 21*, 931-935.

Leiser, D., & Zibershatz, A. (1989). The Traveller: A computational model of spatial network learning. *Environment and Behavior, 21*(4), 435-463.

Levine, M. (1982). You-are-here maps: Psychological considerations. *Environment and Behavior, 14*, 221-237.

Lew, A.A. (1987). English-speaking tourists and the attractions of Singapore. *Singapore Journal of Tropical Geography, 8*, 44-59.

Liben, L.S., & Downs, R.M. (1997). Can-ism and Can'tianism: A straw child. *Annals of the Association of American Geographers, 87*(1), 159-167.

Lockett, C., Boyer-Tarlo, D., & Emonson, J. (1989). Using the floor for exhibit information. *Visitor Studies: Theory, Research and Practice, 2*, 163-167.

Lynch, K. (1960). *The image of the city.* Cambridge, MA: MIT Press & Harvard University Press.

MacEachren, A.M. (1995). *How maps work.* New York: Guildford Press.

Machlis, G. (1992). Interpreting war and peace. In G.E. Machlis & D.R. Field (Eds.), *On interpretation* (pp. 235-244). Corvallis, OR: Oregon State University Press.

Mack, J.A., & Thompson, J.A. (1991). Visitor centre planning: Using visitor interests and available time. In G. Moscardo & K. Hughes (Eds.), *Visitor centres: Exploring new territory* (pp. 113-120). Townsville, Australia: James Cook University.

Manfredo, M.J., & Bright, A.D. (1991). A model for assessing the effects of communication on recreationists. *Journal of Leisure Research, 23*(1), 1-20.

McArthur, S., & Hall, C.M. (1993). Evaluation of visitor management services. In C.M. Hall & S. McArthur (Eds.), *Heritage management in New Zealand and Australia* (pp. 274-278). Auckland, New Zealand: Oxford University Press.

McCleary, G.F., Jr., (1979). Considerations in map use. In *Thematic map design* (pp. 107-108). Cambridge, MA: Harvard University.

McGuire, W.J. (1985). Attitudes and attitude change. In G. Lindzey & E. Aronson (Eds.), *Handbook of Social Psychology*, Vol. 2 (3rd ed.). New York: Random House.

McIntyre, G. (1993). *Sustainable tourism development*. Madrid, Spain: World Tourism Organization.

McManus, P.M. (1987). It's the company you keep... The social determination of learning-related behaviour in a science museum. *The International Journal of Museum Management and Curatorship, 6*, 263-270.

McManus, P.M. (1988). Good companions. More on the social determination of learning-related behaviour in a science museum. *The International Journal of Museum Management and Curatorship, 7*, 37-44.

McManus, P.M. (1989). Oh yes they do: How museum visitors read labels and interact with exhibit texts. *Curator, 32*(3), 174-189.

McManus, P.M. (1994). Families in museums. In R. Miles & L. Zavala (Eds.), *Towards the museum of the future* (pp. 81-96). London: Routledge.

Melton, A.W. (1936). Distribution of attention in galleries in a museum of science and industry. *Museum News, 14*, 5-8.

Miles, R. (1989). *Evaluation in its communications context*. Technical Report No. 89-30. Jacksonville, AL: Center for Social Design.

Miles, R.S., Alt, M.B., Gosling, D.C., Lewis, B.N., & Tout, A.F. (1982). *The design of educational exhibits*. London: George, Allen, & Unwin.

Monmonier, M. (1996). *How to lie with maps* (2nd ed.). Chicago: University of Chicago Press.

Moscardo, G. (1989, September). *Why Johnny won't use the computer*. Paper presented at Museum Educators Association of Australia Annual Conference, Adelaide.

Moscardo, G. (1991). Museum Scripts. *Australian Psychologist, 26*, 158-165.

Moscardo, G. (1992). The tourist-resident distinction: Implications for the management of museums and other interpretive settings. *Journal of Tourism Studies, 3*(2), 2-19.

Moscardo, G. (1993a). *Report on observation of visitors to the Great Barrier Reef Aquarium*. Prepared for the Great Barrier Reef Marine Park Authority.

Moscardo, G. (1993b). *Evaluation of Cradle Mountain visitor centre—final report*. Prepared for the Tasmanian National Parks and Wildlife, Australia.

Moscardo, G. (1996a). Mindful visitors. *Annals of Tourism Research, 23*(2), 376-397.

Moscardo, G. (1996b). Principles for effective interpretation. In *Interpretation in Action* (pp. 7-18). Proceedings of Fifth Annual Interpretation Association Conference, Bendigo, Australia.

Moscardo, G. (1996c). An activities-based segmentation of visitors to Far North Queensland. In G. Prosser (Ed.), *Tourism and Hospitality Research* (pp. 379-395). Canberra, Australia: Bureau of Tourism Research.

Moscardo, G. (1997). Making mindful managers: Evaluating methods for teaching problem solving skills for tourism management. *Journal of Tourism Studies, 8*(1), 16-24.

Moscardo, G., Ditcham, M., Huf, S., Warnett, M., & MacKenzie, K. (1995). Translating wisdom in theory into wisdom in practice. In *Interpretation and the getting of wisdom* (pp. 134-138). Canberra, Australia: Interpretation Australia Association.

Moscardo, G., Woods, B., & Pearce, P. (1997). *Evaluating the effectiveness of pictorial symbols in reef visitor education.* CRC Reef Research Centre Technical Report No. 15. Townsville, Australia: CRC Reef Research Centre.

Moscardo, G., Woods, B., Verbeek, M., & Pearce, P. (1996). *Matching visitor information needs to rainforest interpretation.* Paper presented at the Annual CRC TREM Research Meeting, Kuranda, Australia.

Munson, B.H. (1994). Ecological misconceptions. *Journal of Environmental Education, 25*(4), 30-34.

Myers, D.G. (1986). *Psychology.* New York: Worth Publishers.

Nitsch, B., & van Straaten, J. (1995). Rural tourism development: Using a sustainable tourism development approach. In H. Coccossis & P. Nijkamp (Eds.), *Sustainable Tourism Development* (pp. 127-140). Aldershot, U.K.: Avebury.

Ogden, J.J., Lindburg, D.G., & Maple, T.L. (1993). The effects of ecologically relevant sounds on zoo visitors. *Curator, 36*(2), 147-156.

Oliver, S.S., Roggenbuck, J.W., & Watson, A.E. (1985). Education to reduce impacts in forest campgrounds. *Journal of Forestry, 83*(4), 234-236.

Olsen, E.C., Bowman, M.L., & Roth, R.E. (1984). Interpretation and nonformal education in natural resources management. *Journal of Environmental Education, 15,* 6-10.

O'Neill, M.J. (1991). Evaluation of a conceptual model of architectural legibility. *Environment and Behavior, 23*(3), 259-284.

O'Neill, M.J. (1992). Effects of familiarity and plan complexity on wayfinding in simulated buildings. *Journal of Environmental Psychology, 12,* 319-327.

Orion, N., & Hofstein, A. (1994). Factors that influence learning during a scientific field trip in a natural environment. *Journal of Research in Science Teaching, 31*(10), 1097-1119.

Palij, M., Levine, M., & Kahan, T. (1984). The orientation of cognitive maps. *Bulletin of the Psychonomic Society, 22*(2), 105-108.

Palmerino, M., Langer, E., & McGillis, D. (1984). Attitudes and attitude change: Mindlessness-mindfulness perspective. In J.R. Eiser (Ed.), *Attitudinal judgement* (pp. 179-196). New York: Springer-Verlag.

Pearce, P.L. (1981). Environmental shock: A study of tourists' reactions to two tropical islands. *Journal of Applied Social Psychology, 11(3),* 268-280.

Pearce, P.L. (1982a). *Children's recognition of crocodile warning signs.* Report prepared for Queensland National Parks and Wildlife Service.

Pearce, P.L. (1982b). *The social psychology of tourist behaviour.* Oxford, U.K.: Pergamon Press.

Pearce, P.L. (1984). Tourist-guide interaction. *Annals of Tourism Research, 11,* 129-146.

Pearce, P.L. (1988). *The Ulysses factor: Evaluating visitors in tourist settings.* New York: Springer Verlag.

Pearce, P.L. (1991). Analysing tourist attractions. *Journal of Tourism Studies, 2*(1), 46-55.

Pearce, P.L., & Black, N. (1984). Dimensions of national park maps: A psychological evaluation. *Cartography, 13(3),* 189-203.

Pearce, P.L., & Moscardo, G.M. (1989, June). STAR: The structure of tourist activities for regions. In *Tourism Research: Globalization of the Pacific Rim and beyond.* Proceedings of the Twentieth Tourist and Travel Research Association Conference, Hawaii. Salt Lake City, UT: Graduate School of Business, University of Utah.

Pearce, P.L., Moscardo, G., & Ross, G.F. (1991). Tourism impact and community perception: An equity-social representational perspective. *Australian Psychologist, 26*(3), 147-152.

Pearce, P., Moscardo, G., Green, D., Greenwood, T., Tati, M., & Clark, A. (1997). *Visitor satisfaction at Tjapukai.* Prepared for the Tjapukai Aboriginal Cultural Park.

Peart, B. (1984). Impact of exhibit type on knowledge gain, attitudes, and behavior. *Curator, 27*(3), 220-237.

Petty, R.C., & Cacioppo, J.T. (1981). *Attitudes and persuasion.* Dubuque, IA: Wm. C. Brown.

Petty, R.E., & Cacioppo, J.T. (1986). The elaboration likelihood model of persuasion. *Advances in Experimental Social Psychology, 19,* 123-205.

Petty, R.E., McMichael, S., & Brannon, L. (1992). The elaboration likelihood model of persuasion. In M.J. Manfredo (Ed.), *Influencing human behavior* (pp. 77-102). Champaign, IL: Sagamore Publishing.

Pines, A.L., & West, L.H.T. (1986). Conceptual understanding and science learning. *Science Education, 70,* 583-604.

Poon, A. (1993). *Tourism, technology and competitive strategies.* Wallingford, U.K.: C.A.B. International.

Prince, D.R. (1982). Countryside interpretation: A cognitive evaluation. *Museums Journal, 82,* 165-170.

Rand, J. (1985). *Fish stories that hook readers.* Technical Report No. 90-30. Jacksonville, AL: Centre for Social Design.

Robinson, E.S. (1928). The behaviour of the museum visitor. In P. Bell, J. Fisher, & R. Loomis (1978), *Environmental Psychology.* Philadelphia: W.B. Saunders.

Rodin, J., & Langer, E. (1977). Long-term effects of a control-relevant intervention among the institutionalized aged. *Journal of Personality and Social Psychology, 35,* 897-902.

Roggenbuck, J.W. (1992). Use of persuasion to reduce resource impacts and visitor conflicts. In M.J. Manfredo (Ed.), *Influencing human behavior* (pp. 149-208). Champaign, IL: Sagamore Publishing.

Roggenbuck, J.W., & Williams, D.R. (1991, July). *Commercial tour guides' effectiveness as nature educators.* Paper presented at Leisure and Tourism World Congress, Sydney, Australia.

Rovine, M.J., & Weisman, G.D. (1989). Sketch-map variables as predictors of way-finding performance. *Journal of Environmental Psychology, 9,* 217-232.

Serrell, B. (1977). *Visitor observation studies at the John G. Shedd Aquarium.* Master's thesis, Governors State University.

Sherer, M., & Rogers, D.W. (1984). The role of vivid information in fear appeals and attitude change. *Journal of Research in Personality, 18,* 321-334.

Sholl, M.J. (1992). Landmarks, places, environments. *Geoforum, 23*(2), 151-164.

Shumaker, S.A., & Reizenstein, J.E. (1982). Environmental factors affecting inpatient stress in acute care hospitals. In G.W. Evans (Ed.), *Environmental stress* (pp. 179-223). Cambridge,U.K.: Cambridge University Press.

Simutis, Z.M., & Barsam, H.F. (1983). Terrain visualization and map reading. In H.L. Pick & L.P. Acreddo (Eds.), *Spatial orientation* (pp. 161-194). New York: Plenum Press.

Smith, S.L.J., & Godbey, G.C. (1991). Leisure, recreation and tourism. *Annals of Tourism Research, 18,* 85-100.

Spencer, C., Blades, M., & Morsley, K. (1989). *The child in the physical environment.* Chichester, U.K.: John Wiley & Sons.

Spiegel, G.F., Jr., & Barufaldi, J.P. (1994). The effects of a combination of text structure awareness and graphic postorganizers on recall and retention of science knowledge. *Journal of Research in Science Teaching, 31*(9), 913-932.

Statham, R. (1993). Getting to grips with Japan. *International Journal of Museum Management and Curatorship, 12*(2), 215-219.

Sykes, J.B. (Ed.) (1982). *The Concise Oxford Dictionary.* Oxford, U.K.: Clarendon Press.

Talbot, J.F., Kaplan, R., Kuo, F.E., & Kaplan, S. (1993). Factors that enhance effectiveness of visitor maps. *Environment and Behaviour, 25*(6), 743-760.

Thompson, D., & Bitgood, S. (1988). The effects of sign length, letter size, and proximity on reading. *Visitor Studies: Theory, Research and Practice, 1,* 101-112.

Tilden, F. (1977). *Interpreting our heritage* (3rd ed.). Chapel Hill, NC: University of North Carolina Press.

Tversky, B. (1992). Distortions in cognitive maps. *Geoforum, 23*(2), 131-138.

Tyner, J. (1992). *Introduction to thematic cartography.* Englewood Cliffs, NJ: Prentice Hall.

Urry, J. (1990). *The tourist gaze.* London: Sage.

Uzzell, D.L. (1989). The hot interpretation of war and conflict. In D.L. Uzzell (Ed.), *Heritage interpretation, Volume 1. The natural and built environment* (pp. 33-47). London: Belhaven Press.

Vanderstoep, G.A., & Gramann, J.H. (1987). The effect of verbal appeals and incentives on depreciative behavior among youthful park visitors. *Journal of Leisure Research, 19*(2), 69-83.

Volkert, J.W. (1991). Monologue to dialogue. *Museum News, 70*(2), 46-48.

Walker, E. (1988). A front-end evaluation conducted to facilitate planning the Royal Ontario Museum's European Galleries. *Visitor Studies: Theory, Research and Practice, 1,* 139-143.

Wall, G. (1993). Towards a tourism typology. In J.G. Nelson, R. Butler, & G. Wall (Eds.), *Tourism and sustainable development* (pp. 45-58). Waterloo, Canada: Department of Geography, University of Waterloo.

Walmsley, D.J., & Jenkins, J.M. (1991). Mental maps, locus of control, and activity. *Journal of Tourism Studies, 2*(2), 36-42.

Wandersee, J.H. (1990). Concept mapping and the cartography of cognition. *Journal of Research in Science Teaching, 27*, 923-936.

Warren, D.H. (1994). Self-localization on plan and oblique maps. *Environment and Behavior, 26*(1), 71-98.

Warwick, D.P., & Lininger, C.A. (1975). *The sample survey: Theory and practice.* New York: McGraw-Hill.

Washburne, R.F., & Wagar, J. (1972). Evaluating visitor response to exhibit content. *Curator, 15*, 248-254.

Webb, P., & Wotton, J. (1993). Measuring up to public needs. *Museums Journal, 93*(10), 33.

Wolf, L.F., & Smith, J.K. (1993). What makes museum labels legible? *Curator, 36*(2), 95-110.

Wolf, R.L., & Tymitz, B.L. (1978). *Whatever happened to the Giant Wombat: An investigation of the impact of the Ice Age Mammals and Emergence of Man Exhibit, National Museum of National History, Smithsonian Institution.* Washington, DC: Smithsonian Institution.

Wolf, R.L., & Tymitz, B.L. (1979). *"East side, west side, straight down the middle": A study of visitor perceptions of "Our Changing Land", the Bicentennial exhibit, National Museum of Natural History, Smithsonian Institution.* Washington, D.C.: Smithsonian Institution, Department of Psychological Studies.

Wolf, R.L., & Tymitz, B.L. (1981). *"Hey Mom, that exhibit's alive": A study of visitor perceptions of the Coral Reef Exhibit, National Museum of Natural History, Smithsonian Institution.* Washington, DC: Smithsonian Institution, Museum Evaluation Studies Program, Office of Museum Programs.

Wolf, R.L., Munley, M.E., & Tymitz, B.L. (1979). *The pause that refreshes: A study of visitor reactions to the Discovery Corners in National Museum of History and Technology, Smithsonian Institution.* Washington, DC: Smithsonian Institution, Department of Psychological Studies.

Woods, B., & Moscardo, G. (1996, Oct. 30 - Nov. 2). *Adding value to tourist operations through interpretation.* Paper presented at the 1996 Interpretation Australia Association Conference, Bendigo, Victoria.

Worts, D. (1990). The computer as catalyst: Experiences at the Art Gallery of Ontario. *ILVS Review, 1*(2), 91-108.

Wurman, R.W. (1989). *Information anxiety.* New York: Doubleday.

Zimring, C. (1982). The built environment as a source of psychological stress. In G.W. Evans (Ed.), *Environmental stress* (pp. 151-178). Cambridge, U.K.: Cambridge University Press.

■ Index